Contents

YORK NOTES

General Editors: Professor A.N. Jeffares (*University of Stirling*) & Professor Suheil Bushrui (*American University of Beirut*)

William Shakespeare

THE TAMING OF THE SHREW

Notes by G.M. Ridden

BA M PHIL (LEEDS)
Head of Student Services,
King Alfred's College, Winchester

LONGMAN
YORK PRESS

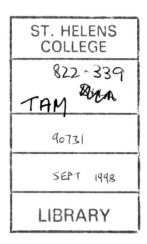
The illustrations of The Globe Playhouse are from
The Globe Restored in Theatre: A Way of Seeing by
Walter C. Hodges, published by Oxford University
Press. © Oxford University Press

YORK PRESS
Immeuble Esseily, Place Riad Solh, Beirut.

ADDISON WESLEY LONGMAN LIMITED
Edinburgh Gate, Harlow,
Essex CM20 2JE, England
Associated companies, branches and representatives
throughout the world

© Librairie du Liban 1981

First published 1981
Eleventh impression 1997

ISBN 0-582-78198-1

Produced by Longman Singapore Publishers Pte Ltd
Printed in Singapore

Part 1

Introduction

Life of William Shakespeare

The baptism of William Shakespeare was recorded on 26 April 1564 in Stratford, England. It is reasonable to assume that he was born not more than a few days before that date. His father, John Shakespeare, was a prominent local citizen who held some of the most important positions in the government of the town. William probably attended Stratford Grammar School but, unlike most other writers of the time, he did not proceed to university. In 1582 he married Anne Hathaway, a lady eight years his senior, and they had three children, the eldest a girl, Susanna, and twins, Hamnet and Judith.

We do not know when or for what reason Shakespeare left Stratford for London, but it is clear that he had established a reputation for himself by 1592 when Robert Greene, a playwright with a university background, warned his learned colleagues against:

> an upstart crow, beautified with our feathers, that with his *tiger's heart wrapped in a player's hide* supposes he is as well able to bombast out a blank verse as the best of you, and being an absolute *Johannes-factotum* is in his own conceit the only Shake-scene in a country.*

It is clear from this attack that Shakespeare was already well known, both as an actor and as a playwright. The following year he published a narrative poem, *Venus and Adonis*, which further enhanced his reputation. He became a shareholder in the theatrical company with which he worked and enjoyed financial as well as professional success, sufficient to allow him to buy in 1597 one of the largest houses in Stratford.

The popularity of Shakespeare's plays is indicated by the description given in 1598 by Francis Meres, who says that they are 'the most excellent in both kinds' (that is, in both tragedies and comedies). Although Shakespeare is not the only playwright mentioned by Meres he is the only one to have his plays listed. Furthermore, after 1598, with the publication of *Love's Labour's Lost*, copies of Shakespeare's plays were regularly published with his name on the title page, a very rare occurrence at that time.

***Greene's Groatsworth of Wit*, quoted in *William Shakespeare, The Complete Works*, edited by Peter Alexander, Collins, London, 1951, p.xvi.

It is not easy to provide accurate dates for all of Shakespeare's thirty-seven plays, but it seems likely that most of his comedies and history plays were written before 1600, that he wrote his great tragedies between 1601 and 1608, and that a few plays requiring more elaborate stage-effects (*Pericles, Cymbeline, The Winter's Tale* and *The Tempest*) were written after the company transferred to a different theatre in 1608.

In the last years of his life Shakespeare lived in retirement in Stratford; he died on 23 April 1616. His wife was buried next to him in 1623.

Elizabethan theatre

There were two distinct and separate kinds of theatre in Shakespeare's time. The private theatres were small, enclosed and socially respectable, an extension of performances given at the royal court. The public theatres were larger, capable of holding audiences of up to two thousand people; they were open to the sky, and not at all respectable.

Before the establishment of either of these kinds of theatre, companies of players would act wherever they could (in the courtyards of inns, for example), competing with other kinds of entertainment such as the dancing of tame bears referred to by Christopher Sly in the Induction of *The Taming of the Shrew*. These strolling players were unpopular with the authorities and, in 1574, London magistrates required that all players and performing areas should be licensed. It was probably as a result of this regulation that the first permanent public theatre was built outside the control of London magistrates in the suburb of Shoreditch in 1576. It was called The Theatre.

The Taming of the Shrew was probably first performed in a public open theatre, circular in shape, with galleries around the side for the more wealthy patrons. These galleries, like the stage itself, were roofed. The majority of the audience, however, sat in the open air around the stage which extended from one wall.

The Taming of the Shrew itself furnishes quite a useful introduction to the Elizabethan public theatre. The device used by the Lord to deceive Sly, providing a boy to act as Sly's 'wife', is based upon the real stage convention of the day that female roles were played by boys. The description of Petruchio's horse in Act III Scene 2 is also necessary, because animals never appeared on the Elizabethan stage.

The Induction requires Sly to enter 'aloft' in the second scene, drawing our attention to the fact that there was a balcony at the rear of the stage, used in other plays for lovers' farewells or for a defiant speech to the crowd. Characters using this balcony were usually of a higher social status than those on the stage below. Beneath this balcony there was a curtained area on each side of which were the doors through which the actors made their entrances and exits. In the case of *The Taming of the*

Shrew one door is to be imagined as the entry into the square, the second as the door to either Lucentio's house or Hortensio's house.

The play also indicates the necessity for a very deep stage, since it often requires one group of characters to stand aside to watch the actions of another group. It may be, also, that at the beginning of Act V Scene 1 Gremio is required to be out at the front of the stage while the action takes place behind his back.

Shakespeare was writing during one of the most flourishing periods in the history of the English theatre. Between 1520 and 1559 only twenty-two plays were registered for publication, whereas in the twenty years after 1559 thirty-five new plays were registered. So popular were

THE GLOBE PLAYHOUSE

The theatre, originally built by James Burbage in 1576, was made of wood (Burbage had been trained as a carpenter). It was situated to the north of the River Thames on Shoreditch in Finsbury Fields. There was trouble with the lease of the land, and so the theatre was dismantled in 1598, and reconstructed 'in another forme' on the south side of the Thames as the Globe. Its sign is thought to have been a figure of the Greek hero Hercules carrying the globe. It was built in six months, its galleries being roofed with thatch. This caught fire in 1613 when some smouldering wadding, from a cannon used in a performance of Shakespeare's *Henry VIII*, lodged in it. The theatre was burnt down, and when it was rebuilt again on the old foundations, the galleries were roofed with tiles.

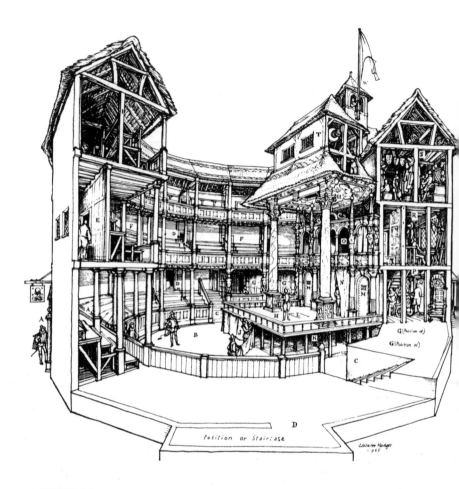

A CONJECTURAL RECONSTRUCTION OF THE INTERIOR OF THE GLOBE PLAYHOUSE

AA Main entrance
 B The Yard
CC Entrances to lowest gallery
 D Entrance to staircase and upper galleries
 E Corridor serving the different sections of the middle gallery
 F Middle gallery ('Twopenny Rooms')
 G 'Gentlemen's Rooms' or Lords' Rooms'
 H The stage
 J The hanging being put up round the stage
 K The 'Hell' under the stage
 L The stage trap, leading down to the Hell
MM Stage doors

 N Curtained 'place behind the stage'
 O Gallery above the stage, used as required sometimes by musicians, sometimes by spectators, and often as part of the play
 P Back-stage area (the tiring-house)
 Q Tiring-house door
 R Dressing-rooms
 S Wardrobe and storage
 T The hut housing the machine for lowering enthroned gods, etc., to the stage
 U The 'Heavens'
 W Hoisting the playhouse flag

the theatres that the traveller Fynes Morrison wrote in 1617 that there were in London 'four or five companies of players with their peculiar theatres capable of holding many thousands, wherein they all play every day in the week except Sunday'.*

Shakespeare's comedies

When Shakespeare's plays were first published together in 1623 they were divided into three categories: comedy, history and tragedy. Of the three, comedy is perhaps the most difficult to describe and define. The origins of Elizabethan comedy lie way back in classical antiquity, as do those of many of the literary genres of this period, and the form developed from Greek to Roman and into Italian comedy before reaching the Elizabethan stage.

Early classical comedy was often bawdy and unsophisticated. Its humour generally arose from the farcical actions of the characters, and there was little attempt to examine the motives or personalities behind those actions. The audience would laugh at the folly of the characters on stage and at the visual spectacle of slaves being beaten by their masters or ardent lovers being denied the opportunity to get into bed. Very often these follies would reflect some prevalent vice of the time, and one function of this early variety of comedy was to satirise either social or political targets. The plots were usually concerned with illicit sexual liaisons, often at the expense of old husbands unable to carry out their fantasies. The relationship between men and women was rarely depicted as an ennobling force in these early comedies, but rather as a passion which drove men to ridiculous behaviour. Sometimes even the gods of classical mythology were included in the drama, degraded and made ludicrous by love.

As comedy developed it became more sophisticated and devoted more of its attention to the kinds of intrigues and deceits used by lovers to obtain their desires. An element in this stage of development is the growth in the significance of servant characters. Very often these servants are wily and resourceful, carrying out the intrigues on behalf of their masters. The plots of the comedies became more complex, sometimes adding to the confusion by including a pair of identical twins, having one character disguised as another, or introducing conflicts within a family (for example, between an old husband and a young wife, or between a tyrannical father and his children). As we move towards Shakespearean comedy the concern of the plays moves away from illicit sex towards a more romantic version of courtship which inevitably ends in marriage.

*quoted in Leo Salingar, *Shakespeare and the Traditions of Comedy*, Cambridge University Press, Cambridge, 1974, p.259.

Shakespeare's comedies are not about adulterous or unwedded love and, indeed, in the one play which features prominently a pair of lovers who have been to bed before their wedding (*Measure for Measure*), the punishment which is inflicted upon them for this 'crime' brings the play perilously close to becoming a tragedy. A complex courtship leading ultimately to marriage is a very common basic theme for a Shakespearean comedy, and, when the marriages at the end of *Love's Labour's Lost* are postponed, Berowne draws attention to the way in which this frustrates the audience's expectation of the way in which a comedy should end:

> Our wooing doth not end like an old play
> Jack hath not Jill: these ladies' courtesy
> Might well have made our sport a comedy. (V.2.866-9)

One element of comedy which is preserved from classical times through to the Elizabethan period is its ritual significance. Plays have always been associated with holidays and carnivals as an appropriate way of relaxing on days when no work needed to be done. Very often other kinds of entertainment, such as feasting, drinking and dancing, were also involved with these holidays, and these were probably occasions when the normal barriers of social class were ignored or even reversed. Thus, for example, we find holidays when it was the tradition for the master of the house to wait upon his servants, or for one of the servants to be elected 'master' for the day to preside over the festivities. This element of holiday merriment, with a temporary lord in charge of the revels, is well reflected in Shakespeare's comedies. Christopher Sly, when told that the players are to act for him a comedy, exclaims:

> Is not a comonty a Christmas gambold or a tumbling-trick?
> (Induction 2, 135-6)

He knows the connection between comedy and holiday, and the fact that it might end with a 'tumble' in his bed with his new 'wife'. *Twelfth Night* actually takes its title from one of the principal occasions for enjoyment in the Christmas calendar and the activity at the house of Lady Olivia is like a rowdy party presided over by Sir Toby Belch. Ultimately, of course, all parties must end, and the normal social conventions need to be reasserted, confusions are unravelled, and the entertainment is over for another year.

It is clear from reading Elizabethan comedies, and more especially contemporary critics writing about those comedies, that Shakespeare's work is superior to that of any other playwright of his day. One particular vice of many Elizabethan plays is that, because they were derived from lengthy prose romances which had their heroes travelling long distances over many years in search of lost children or lovers, they frequently stretched the credibility of their audiences to an unacceptable degree. Stephen Gosson wrote in 1580 in *Plays Confuted*:

> Sometime you shall see nothing but the adventures of an amorous knight, passing from country to country for the love of his lady, encountering many a terrible monster made of brown paper, and at his return, is so wonderfully changed, that he cannot be known but by some posy in his Tablet, or by a broken ring.

In contrast, Shakespeare's comedies are remarkable for their unity: characters in his plays may have travelled and had adventures, but these journeys are reported and have usually taken place before the action of the play itself begins. There are very few changes of location in his comedies and certainly nothing approaching the complexities ridiculed by Sir Philip Sidney:

> You shall have Asia of the one side, and Afric of the other, and so many other under-kingdoms, that the player, when he cometh in, must ever begin with telling where he is. . . . Now you shall have three Ladies walk to gather flowers: and then we must believe the stage to be a Garden. By and by we hear news of shipwreck in the same place: and then we are to blame if we accept it not for a rock. . . . Now, of time they are much more liberal: for ordinary it is that two young princes fall in love; after many traverses, she is got with child, delivered of a fair boy; he is lost, groweth a man, and is ready to get another child; and all this in two hours' space.*

Sidney goes on in this same pamphlet to contrast the ridiculousness of English comedies with the current practice among 'the ordinary players in Italy' which he much prefers. Shakespeare would not need to know Italian in order to be aware of the practices and plots of Italian comedies: these were available in French and English translations. Furthermore, the principal contribution of Italian comedy was not a literary contribution at all, but came through the techniques of acting developed in the branch of comedy known as the *commedia dell' arte*. This kind of comedy relied on the abilities of professional actors to improvise and display their skills around a standard plot. As in other kinds of comedy, the story centred on the adventures of young lovers who tricked their elders and were aided by skilful servants. Some of the standard figures from the *commedia dell' arte* are referred to in *Love's Labour's Lost*: 'The pedant, the braggart, the hedge-priest, the fool and the boy' (V.2.536); and the treatment of certain characters in his comedies (especially in *The Taming of the Shrew*) owes a great deal to the Italian tradition.

* A Defence of Poetry, edited by Jan van Dorsten, Oxford University Press, London, 1966, pp.65–6.

Love and marriage

As we have seen, Shakespeare's comedies are generally concerned with courtship and marriage, and it is possible to distinguish three different attitudes to love in the Elizabethan period: two literary traditions, plus the reality of contemporary life.

The Roman poet Ovid (43BC–AD18) is in part responsible for both of the literary traditions. His humorous work *The Art of Love* was adopted by medieval courtiers as if it were a serious statement of the way in which a lady ought to be wooed. It describes an elaborate ritual of courtship in which the man was always inferior to the lady, swearing to be ever faithful to her, suffering, sighing and even dying for her: all without any hope of ever attaining her love. In the medieval courts of Southern France the lady of the castle really did exercise power over the knights: she was second only to the lord himself and the knights would direct their devotion and their songs of love to the lady. Thus evolved a literary tradition known as 'courtly love', in which poets wrote of their pain in loving distant, unattainable and perfect ladies. In England this tradition developed into a convention of courtship in which the lover's pain was finally cured by his marriage to the lady. The tradition is reflected at its finest in Geoffrey Chaucer's (1340–1400) *Troilus and Criseyde* (1380–6).

Ovid, however, had also written another kind of poetry in which a very different view of the relationship between men and women is reflected. In his *Elegies* he described in detail the kinds of affairs and liaisons actually practised in the Roman society of his day. Here the lover, in sharp contrast to the lover of the courtly tradition, was usually able to enjoy his lady physically and, if a particular lady was unwilling to yield to him, he did not suffer and die but simply directed his attentions elsewhere. In his *Metamorphoses* Ovid wrote of the adventures of the mythological gods when they fell in love. In both the *Elegies* and the *Metamorphoses* a far more frank and explicit portrait of love was given than in the courtly love tradition. Sexual love was described in detail and with some humour. Both men and gods are described in Ovidian poetry as made ridiculous by their love. Shakespeare himself wrote a narrative poem in this tradition (*Venus and Adonis*) in which the goddess Venus has all the baser characteristics of a human being and is degraded by her love. In contrast the lover in the courtly love tradition expected to be elevated by his devotion to his lady, and to acquire some control and mastery over his human weaknesses.

The reality of marriage in Elizabethan times was different from both of the two literary conventions outlined above. The husband expected his wife to be completely obedient to his will and looked for absolute supremacy over her. Marriages were often arranged for very unromantic reasons: to strengthen political alliances, to improve social standing, to provide old men with heirs to their estates, to provide impoverished suitors with wealth through a large dowry.

Thus a paradox arose. A man might use the convention of courtly love to win his lady, but after marriage treat her as an inferior, a piece of property. Sir Thomas Wyatt (1503–42), the writer of some of the finest of English courtly love lyrics, advised his newly married son, 'rule well and honestly your wife as your fellow, and she shall love and reverence you as her head'.* Even the Bible seemed to offer contradictory advice for on the one hand the reverence due to the Virgin Mary might seem to argue for the superiority of woman, while on the other hand it was through a woman, Eve, that Paradise was lost. Contemporary writers tended to agree with St Paul's view in Ephesians 5:22–4, 'Let women be subject to their husbands, as to the Lord; for the husband is the head of the woman, as Christ is the head of the Church'.

From the medieval period onwards we find women in literature who are unwilling to accept the superiority of their husbands and who become figures of fun, 'shrews' who must eventually be taught a lesson. The character of Noah's wife in medieval drama is one of the earliest examples of a scolding wife, and the most extensive treatment of the debate over superiority in marriage comes in Chaucer's *Canterbury Tales*, centring on the Wife of Bath.

A note on the text

Fourteen of Shakespeare's plays were published during his lifetime in books called quartos. In addition certain plays were published in imperfect versions remembered either by the actors or by members of the audience who tried to reconstruct what they had seen. *The Taming of the Shrew* was not published in Shakespeare's lifetime, although a different play entitled *The Taming of a Shrew* was published in 1594; this may be an imperfect version of Shakespeare's play reconstructed from memory by a member of the audience.

The first published version of Shakespeare's *The Taming of the Shrew* was in the First Folio, a collected edition of all the plays thought to have been written by Shakespeare, published by the actors Heminge and Condell in 1623. Modern editions are based upon this First Folio edition. The line references in this present set of notes are to *The Taming of the Shrew*, edited by G.R. Hibbard in the New Penguin Shakespeare series, Penguin Books, Harmondsworth, 1968. If you use a different edition you should have no difficulty in identifying passages referred to in the notes since the variation in line numbering will be very slight.

* quoted in Patricia Thomson, *Sir Thomas Wyatt and his Background*, Stanford University Press, Stanford, 1964, p.10.

Part 2

Summaries

of THE TAMING OF THE SHREW

A general summary

Christopher Sly, a drunkard, is found asleep by a Lord who takes him
into his house and has him treated as a nobleman. For Sly's entertainment a play is presented which concerns the courtship and marriage of
the two daughters of Baptista Minola, a wealthy Italian. Baptista insists
that his younger daughter Bianca, who has two suitors, may not marry
until a husband is found for her hot-tempered sister Katherina. Bianca's
suitors, Gremio and Hortensio, agree to help to find a husband for
Katherina and to win Baptista's favour by finding a tutor for Bianca.
Lucentio arrives with his servant Tranio, falls in love with Bianca, and
devises a scheme to win her by changing clothes with Tranio and getting
himself engaged to teach Bianca. Petruchio, a friend of Hortensio, who
is looking for a wealthy wife, is persuaded to woo Katherina and to
present the disguised Hortensio as another tutor for Bianca. Lucentio,
however, wins her heart. Petruchio courts Katherina very roughly and
marries her, although he behaves oddly at the wedding and immediately
rushes off with his bride. At his home Petruchio tames Katherina and
she is forced to acknowledge his superiority. Baptista, meanwhile, has
promised to marry Bianca to Tranio, whom he believes to be the
wealthy Lucentio, and Tranio has advanced this plot by persuading an
old man to pose as his father and to promise Baptista a large dowry.
The real Lucentio marries Bianca in secret and the confusion is height-
ened when Lucentio's real father arrives. However, all ends happily and,
at the final wedding feast, Petruchio proves that the reformed Katherina
is a more obedient wife than either Bianca or the widow whom Hortensio has married.

Detailed summaries

Induction Scene 1

Christopher Sly argues with the hostess of the Inn and lies in a drunken
sleep on the ground. He is found by a lord who is returning from hunting
and who decides to trick Sly by having him carried into his house and
dressed as a nobleman. A band of strolling actors arrives and the lord

arranges that they shall perform for Sly when he wakes, and that a
pageboy is to impersonate Sly's wife.

NOTES AND GLOSSARY:

Induction:	a scene or group of scenes which introduce or lead into the main action
pheeze:	(*dialect*) destroy
rogue:	Sly is offended at being called a rogue (a peasant) and claims noble ancestors
Richard Conqueror:	unfortunately Sly is too ignorant to avoid confusing William the Conqueror and Richard Lionheart
paucas pallabris:	(rather poor *Spanish*) 'few words'
let the world slide:	do not worry
Sessa:	be quiet
denier:	a very small coin
Go by, Saint Jeronimy:	Sly misquotes a line from a very popular play of the time, Kyd's *The Spanish Tragedy*
thirdborough:	constable
boy:	servant
and kindly:	by all means
tender well:	look after
Breathe:	rest
embossed:	foaming with exhaustion
brach:	female dog
in the coldest fault:	with the poorest of scents
practise on:	play a trick upon
brave:	finely dressed
wanton:	decorative, alluring
procure me:	obtain. The 'me' is redundant
ewer:	water-jug
diaper:	towel
Kindly:	well, as if it were natural
passing excellent:	very excellent
husbanded with modesty:	carried out without excess
As he shall think:	so that he will think
Sirrah:	the common form of address used by a master to a servant
Belike:	perhaps
An't please:	if you please
So please:	if it pleases
Soto:	it is not clear to which play this reference alludes. There is a character called Soto in a later play by John Fletcher

in happy time:	at a fortunate time
The rather:	especially, all the more so
modesties:	ability to restrain yourselves
over-eyeing of:	perceiving
yet his honour . . . play:	the lord perhaps does Sly a disservice here, since Sly's allusion to *The Spanish Tragedy* above might suggest some acquaintance with drama
the veriest antic:	the most oddly behaved person
the buttery:	the room where liquid refreshments were served
want nothing:	lack nothing
in all suits:	(a) in all respects, (b) in all clothing. There is added humour in this speech because the female roles in Elizabethan plays were always played by boys
He bear himself:	he must bear himself
'What is't your honour . . . her love?':	the page is to impersonate a conventional, submissive wife—the role that Katherina is tamed into accepting in the main action of the play
this seven years:	the length of Sly's 'sickness' is extended by the servants in the next scene to fifteen years
esteemed him:	believed himself to be
such a shift:	such a purpose
in despite:	inevitably
Anon:	then
Haply:	perhaps
spleen:	urge to laugh aloud

Induction Scene 2

Sly is treated as a nobleman by the lord and his servants and reluctantly accepts his new identity. Bartholomew the page is introduced as Sly's wife and Sly's desire to take his 'wife' straight to bed is thwarted by the entry of the players and the start of the main action.

NOTES AND GLOSSARY:

small ale:	the cheapest kind of beer
sack:	Spanish wine, the drink of a gentleman
conserves:	candied fruit
conserves of beef:	salted beef
overleather:	the upper part of the shoe
old Sly's son of Burton-heath:	this scene is full of references to Shakespeare's own country of Warwickshire
pedlar:	wandering trader
cardmaker:	maker of combs used in spinning wool

bear-herd: one who leads a performing bear

tinker: a mender of pots and pans

on the score: in debt

sheer ale: ale alone, without any food

beck: command

Apollo: the Greek god of music

Semiramis: an Assyrian goddess of legendary beauty

trapped: ornamented

welkin: a poetic word for the sky

course: hunt with greyhounds

breathed: strong-winded

Adonis painted ... tears are drawn: these descriptions are probably not of any actual paintings. All describe mortals who were loved by gods, and the changes brought about by that love. The stories behind these pictures are all to be found in Ovid (see p.18)

Adonis: in classical mythology, a young huntsman loved by Venus (Cytherea) and changed into a flower. Shakespeare's first published work was the poem *Venus and Adonis*

wanton: sway

Io: in classical mythology, a maiden pursued by Jupiter and changed into a heifer

lively: vividly

Daphne: in classical mythology, a maiden pursued by Apollo and turned into a laurel

waning age: decadent time

By my fay: by my faith (an oath)

goodly: considerable

present her at the leet: charge her at the assizes

stone jugs and no sealed quarts: sealed quarts were officially stamped and held a guaranteed full measure. Stone jugs were not of a standard size

Marry: truly

I fare well: I am well, or I have good food

goodman: the peasant word for 'husband'

abandoned: excluded

it stands so: a bawdy allusion to Sly's aroused lust

the flesh and the blood: desire

congealed your blood: it was believed that all physical and mental disorders were related to the condition of the blood

frenzy: mental illness

they thought it good you hear a play: recreation and the visiting of plays were often prescribed as a cure for melancholy

comonty:	comedy. Sly, like many of Shakespeare's foolish characters, mispronounces words
gambold:	dance
tumbling trick ... household stuff:	there are probably bawdy innuendoes here, following Sly's desire to get his 'wife' to bed. Both 'tumble' and 'stuff' can be used in this sense
history:	story

Act I Scene 1

Lucentio has come to Padua to study, accompanied by his servant Tranio. They watch as Baptista explains to Gremio and Hortensio that they may not court Bianca until her sister Katherina is wed. Gremio and Hortensio agree to postpone their rivalry until they have found a suitor for Katherina, and to try to please Baptista by engaging a tutor for Bianca. Lucentio, meanwhile, has fallen in love with Bianca and decides with Tranio that his best strategy is to be hired as her tutor. Tranio and Lucentio exchange clothes and persuade Biondello, another servant, to support their trick. Sly comments on his enjoyment of the play.

NOTES AND GLOSSARY:

Padua, nursery of arts:	there was a university at Padua from 1228 onwards
for:	in
breathe:	rest
ingenious:	academic
for the time:	at present
plash:	puddle
with satiety:	by filling himself
Mi perdonato:	(*Italian*) pardon me
effected as:	of the same opinion as
stoics ... stocks:	Tranio urges his master not to avoid all pleasure while he studies and to become a 'stoic' (one who despises pleasure) or a 'stock' (an unfeeling stick)
devote:	devoted
checks:	restraints
Ovid:	Publius Ovidius Naso (43BC–AD18), a Roman poet celebrated mainly for his amorous poetry
Balk:	use in conversation
logic ... stomach serves you:	Tranio reviews the major branches of an academic curriculum—rhetoric, mathematics, music, poetry and metaphysics, and urges that each of these be studied in a pleasurable way

stomach:	appetite, desire
ta'en:	taken
affect:	desire
Gramercies:	thanks
come ashore:	Shakespeare seems to think that Padua is a sea-port
Enter . . . Gremio, a pantaloon:	Pantaloon was one of the standard characters of Italian comedy, a ridiculous old man who is an obstacle to the young lovers
some show:	Lucentio and Tranio become an audience, watching the other characters as an audience watches a play
bestow:	find a husband for
cart her:	prostitutes were punished by being carried round in a cart. There is a pun here on 'court' in the previous line
stale:	(a) a laughing-stock, (b) a harlot, sold to the highest bidder
mates:	low fellows
no mates for you:	(a) no husbands for you, (b) not similar to you
I' faith:	certainly
I wis:	truly
it is not halfway to her heart:	marriage is not something which she (Katherina herself) takes seriously
comb your noddle:	beat your head
froward:	perverse (a key word in the play)
Mum:	quiet
peat:	pet, favourite child
It is best . . . know why:	if she could think of a reason her best plan would be to make herself weep
Minerva:	the Roman goddess of wisdom
strange:	unnatural
mew her up:	imprison her
for:	because of
make her . . . tongue:	make Bianca be punished for Katherina's shrewishness
Prefer them:	recommend them
cunning:	knowledgeable
belike:	perhaps
dam:	mother
Love is not . . . fairly out:	love is not so important to prevent us waiting patiently together for things to improve
Our cake's . . . sides:	there is no profit whatsoever for us
wish him:	recommend him
parle:	negotiation between us
toucheth us both:	is to the advantage of both of us

Marry: truly

so very a fool: so complete a fool

alarums: trumpets of war signalling the beginning of a battle

an: if

as lief: as willingly

small choice in rotten apples: that is, no choice at all

bar in law: legal obstacle (Baptista's refusal to allow Bianca to be courted)

have to't: renew our rivalry

Happy man be his dole: may the best man win

of a sudden: suddenly

love in idleness: love striking while one least suspects. This phrase is also the popular name of a flower, the pansy

as secret: as much in my confidence

Anna: sister and confidante of Dido, Queen of Carthage, a character in the Latin epic, the *Aeneid*, by Virgil (70–19BC)

I burn, I pine, I perish: this kind of extreme language is typical of the courtly lover

Affection . . . heart: your love will not be driven from your heart by my scolding

Redime te captum quam queas minimo: (*Latin*) release yourself from captivity as cheaply as you can—a quotation from *The Eunuch*, a play by the Latin dramatist Terence (194–158BC); he was a Roman citizen, born in Carthage

Go forward: give me more advice

the pith: the central issue

the daughter of Agenor: in classical mythology, Europa, beloved of Jove, who carried her off in the disguise of a bull. Another Ovidian tale

her coral lips: that is, Bianca's

curst: perverse

shrewd: difficult to control

mewed her up: imprisoned her

Because: so that

'tis plotted: I have a plan

meet and jump in one: are the very same

bear your part: take your place

Basta: (*Italian*) enough

port: style of living

Uncase thee: take off your cloak

sith: since

tied: obliged

Lucentio loves:	Lucentio is in love
be a slave:	Lucentio has to adopt a lower social status to win his love
thralled:	captivated: again an expression typical of the language of courtly love
descried:	recognised
as becomes:	as is appropriate
Ne'er a whit:	not at all
execute:	carry out
nod:	fall asleep
mind:	pay attention to
Would:	I wish

Act I Scene 2

Petruchio arrives from Verona with his servant Grumio to visit his friend Hortensio. Petruchio tells Hortensio that he has come to seek a wife and Hortensio offers to introduce him to the shrewish Katherina. In addition, Hortensio decides to disguise himself and to have Petruchio present him as a tutor for Bianca. At this point Gremio enters with the disguised Lucentio, whom he has engaged as a tutor to plead his case for Bianca. Finally the disguised Tranio arrives to offer himself as another 'suitor' for Bianca. Hortensio, Gremio and Tranio agree to pay Petruchio's expenses in his wooing of Katherina.

NOTES AND GLOSSARY:

I trow:	I believe
rebused:	Grumio, like Sly, mispronounces words: he means 'abused'
knock me here:	the confusion which occurs here between master and servant is a result of Petruchio's use of 'knock me'. The 'me' is redundant, and is not an invitation for Grumio to beat Petruchio. See 'Swinge me them' in V.2.103
pate:	head
I should knock:	if I were to knock
an:	if
ring it:	(a) ring the doorbell, (b) wring Grumio's ears
sol-fa:	sing the notes of the scale
fray:	quarrel
Con tutto . . . trovato:	(*Italian*) with all my heart, well met
Alla nostra . . . Petruchio:	(*Italian*) welcome to our house, most honoured Petruchio
compound:	settle

'leges:	alleges
in Latin:	Grumio is so English a servant that he does not even know the difference between Italian and Latin
two and thirty, a pip out:	quite mad
I am Grumio's pledge:	I will protect Grumio
heavy chance:	unfortunate occurrence
happy gale:	fortunate wind (again a metaphor suggesting that Padua is a sea-port)
farther:	elsewhere
in a few:	in a few words
maze:	quest
Haply:	if I am lucky
roundly:	frankly
burden:	the chorus, refrain of a tune
Florentius' love:	Florentius in John Gower's (1325–1408) *Confessio Amantis* (1383–4) is forced to marry an old hag who subsequently turns into a most beautiful young woman. Chaucer used this story in *The Wife of Bath's Tale*
Sibyl:	a prophetess in Greek legend, traditionally regarded as very old
Xanthippe:	wife of the Greek philosopher Socrates
moves:	discourages
as rough . . . seas:	images of sea-voyages are a common feature of Petruchio's style
to wive it:	to find a wife
aglet-baby:	a doll
trot:	hag
diseases . . . horses:	Petruchio himself rides a diseased horse in III.2
withal:	as well
are stepped thus far in:	have gone so far
that I broached:	what I touched upon
board her:	woo her (as a sea-captain captures a ship by boarding it)
I will not sleep:	perhaps an ironic anticipation of the way in which Petruchio is to tame Katherina by depriving her of sleep
give you over:	abandon your company
O' my word:	upon my word
an:	if
rope-tricks:	rhetoric—another word Grumio mispronounces. Rhetoric was an academic subject, one which Petruchio puts to practical use
an she but stand:	if she resists

throw a figure: (a) reply with a 'figure' from rhetoric, (b) cast a magic spell

no more eyes to see than a cat: an intricate joke including a pun on Kate/ Cat as well as an allusion to the cat o' nine tails, the whip that might normally be used to tame shrewish wives

keep: custody

do me grace: do me a favour

offer me: present me

by herself: alone

A proper ... amorous: Grumio comments ironically on the inappropriateness of old Gremio as a suitor

note: list of books

mend it with a largess: increase it with a further payment

have them: have the books

stand you so assured: you may be assured

woodcock: a bird easy to catch and hence considered stupid

mum: be quiet

Trow you: do you know

help me to another: introduce me to another. The 'other' to which Hortensio refers is, of course, himself in the disguise of Licio

bags: money bags

vent our love: argue about who loves most

indifferent: equally

Upon ... liking: if we will make a financial settlement which he considers sufficient

please: is sufficient

say'st me so: an expression of disbelief

such a life ... strange: it would be difficult to have 'good days' with a wife like Katherina

a stomach: such an inclination

to't a God's name: get on with it, for God's sake

Will I live?: as surely as I will live

ordnance: artillery

'larums: alarums, trumpets of war

a chestnut in a farmer's fire: chestnuts, when roasted, explode

Tush: no

fear boys with bugs: frighten children with tales of bogey-men

happily: fortunately

whatsoe'er: whatever it might amount to

bravely dressed: dressed like a gentleman

He that has ... mean?: Biondello and Tranio have rehearsed their lines before entering in their new roles

you mean not her: you do not intend to woo Bianca

What have you to do?: what business is it of yours?

Not her that chides: you do not intend to woo the sister that chides (Katherina)

If you be gentlemen: the irony is that, while Gremio and Hortensio are gentlemen, Tranio is not

this right: this courtesy

Leda's daughter: Helen of Troy, married to Menelaus, King of Sparta. She ran away with Paris, a son of Priam, King of Troy. This caused the Trojan War which ended in the fall of Troy after a long siege by the Greeks. They finally took it by the stratagem of the wooden horse

Then well . . . Bianca have: so it is appropriate that Bianca should have one more wooer than she already has

Though Paris came: even if Paris himself were to come

in hope to speed: hoping to succeed

give him his head, I know he'll prove a jade: let him carry on, he'll soon tire himself out. Two metaphors taken from horse-riding

labour . . . Alcides twelve: Hercules (Alcides) the Greek mythological hero had twelve super-human tasks (labours) to perform

hearken for: wait upon

then is free: at that point will be free

stead: benefit

For our access: so that we may be free to woo her

whose hap . . . ingrate: whoever is fortunate enough to win Bianca will not be so unmannerly as to fail to reward you

conceive: understand

gratify this gentleman: pay Petruchio

contrive: pass away

motion: suggestion. The servants adopt the language of their masters

ben venuto: (*Italian*) host

Act II Scene 1

Bianca, whose wrists have been tied by Katherina, is released by her father. The suitors arrive to introduce Petruchio, the 'tutors' and the disguised Tranio to Baptista. Baptista and Petruchio discuss the wooing of Katherina, while Hortensio, in the guise of the tutor Licio, has his 'head broken' by Katherina as he tries to teach her to play the lute. Katherina and Petruchio finally meet and he woos her very roughly and rudely, swearing he will tame her. When Baptista, Gremio and Tranio re-enter Petruchio announces that he has won Katherina, although her behaviour seems to indicate the very opposite. The date of their wedding is fixed for the following Sunday and Petruchio leaves for home to make preparations. Tranio and Gremio negotiate with Baptista for Bianca's hand and the disguised Tranio is able to outbid Gremio. However, he is required to produce a father to guarantee the dowry which he promises.

NOTES AND GLOSSARY:

gauds:	ornaments
dissemble:	deceive
minion:	favourite
affect him:	are fond of him
belike:	perhaps
fair:	well dressed
envy:	hate
ply thy needle:	do your embroidery—an appropriate activity for a lady
hilding:	baggage
in my sight:	in my presence
suffer me:	allow me to do as I wish

dance barefoot on her wedding-day: a humiliating custom

lead apes in hell: the proverbial fate of an unmarried woman

disguised as Cambio: the name Cambio means 'exchange'

hearing of her beauty . . . behaviour: this is one of the occasions on which Petruchio pretends to believe a situation which he knows to be untrue

bashful:	shy
Am bold:	intend

entrance . . . entertainment: a metaphor from the playhouse. Petruchio offers the disguised Hortensio as his entrance fee

Accept of him:	the 'of' is redundant
not for your turn:	unsuitable for you
Saving your tale:	with respect
Baccare:	(corrupt *Latin*) stand back

would fain be doing: wish to get on with business

curse:	prejudice: 'Curse' is clearly a key word in the play
grateful:	welcome

walk like a stranger: stand apart from the rest of the company

the preferment of:	the allowing of a prior claim to
instrument:	that is, the lute

If you accept . . . great: a nicely turned compliment—Tranio, though not a gentleman, can speak like one

presently:	immediately
use them:	treat them
passing welcome:	very welcome
in possession:	at the time of the wedding
Her widowhood:	the right to my property after my death
specialities:	contracts
covenants:	promises
special thing:	major requirement
all in all:	essential
happy be thy speed:	may you be successful
to the proof:	so as to be proof against them
prove a soldier:	(a) become a soldier, (b) put a soldier to the test
break her to the lute:	teach her to play the lute. To 'break' a wild horse is to tame it
frets:	(a) the divisions on the fingerboard of a lute, (b) causes for bad temper
fume:	rage
pate:	head
pillory:	an instrument of chastisement in which the head and wrists were locked between two boards
twangling Jack:	an unmusical fool
As had she studied:	as if she had deliberately set out
lusty wench:	spirited girl
go with me:	spoken to Hortensio
good turns:	good lessons
Say that she rail:	if she rants
volubility:	tone of voice
the banns:	the announcement of the wedding
Kate:	Petruchio uses the abbreviated form of her name—impolite on a first meeting
in faith:	in truth
plain Kate:	(a) just Kate, (b) Kate the unbeautiful
dainties are all Kates:	a pun on the meaning of 'kate', a cake
sounded:	described
movable:	piece of furniture
sit on me:	an improper suggestion
Women are made to bear:	that is, to have children
jade:	an old, weary creature
a swain:	a country fool
Should be? Should—buzz!:	a complicated joke which gives Petruchio the opportunity to steal a kiss from Katherina. 'Be' is identical in sound to 'bee', the creature which makes a buzzing noise, and to 'buss' is to kiss
ta'en:	caught

buzzard: (a) a stupid person, (b) a bird of prey

turtle: turtle-dove, the symbol of love

Ay, for a turtle . . . buzzard: there is no clear explanation for this line

tongue in your tail: an obscene innuendo

try: test out

cuff: beat

arms: (a) heraldic symbol of a gentleman, a coat of arms, (b) limbs

A herald, Kate?: Do you know about heraldry, Kate?

put me in thy books: register me as a gentleman in your heraldic book

a coxcomb: the symbol of foolishness

a crab: a bad-tempered person

a glass: a mirror

In sooth, you scape not so: truly, you will not escape like this

passing gentle: very gentle

gamesome: fond of jests

askance: disdainfully

halt: limp

and whom thou keep'st command: give orders to those whom you employ

Dian: Diana, the Greek goddess of chastity

become: adorn

extempore: improvised

mother-wit: natural intelligence

A witty mother . . .son: if your mother had not been witty her son would have been a fool

keep you warm: you have enough intelligence to keep yourself warm

Marry, so I mean: that is exactly what I intend

chat: idle talk

'greed: agreed

wil you, nill you: whether you like it or not

a husband for your turn: an appropriate husband for you

a wild Kate: a wildcat

conformable: placid

household Kates: domestic cats

how speed you: how are you getting on

In your dumps?: are you in a melancholy mood?

Jack: rough fellow

Father: Petruchio had already (line 130) addressed Baptista as if the marriage had taken place

for policy: as a strategy

Grissel: the story of Patient Griselda, the paragon of wifely obedience, is found in Chaucer's *Clerk's Tale*

Lucrece: the subject of a poem, *The Rape of Lucrece*, by Shakespeare (1594)

goodnight our part: we can say farewell to our hope of wooing Bianca

'twixt us twain, being alone: between the two of us; when we're alone

vied: redoubled

meacock: timid

'gainst: in preparation for

fine: well dressed

Sunday comes apace: Sunday will soon be here

clapped up: put together

venture madly on a desperate mart: a metaphor from trading—Baptista is risking his treasure (Katherina) in a risky enterprise

fretting by you: (a) gaining no interest (continuing the metaphor of trade), (b) annoying you

Youngling: boy, novice. This battle of words between Gremio and Tranio centres on the difference in their ages

Skipper: half-wit

compound: settle

deeds must win the prize: this is ironic, since Tranio wins the victory in this scene on the basis of false words rather than deeds

greatest dower: the financial arrangements for the marriage of Bianca are different from those made for Katherina: see below, p.54

plate: silver

ewers: jugs

lave: wash

Tyrian: a rich and expensive purple cloth

arras counterpoints: bedspreads of tapestry made in Arras, in northern France

bossed: decorated

milch-kine to the pail: dairy cows

answerable to this portion: corresponding to an estate of this size

struck: old

jointure: estate when I am dead

pinched: beaten

argosy: merchant ship

lying in Marseilles road: anchored at Marseilles

galliases . . . galleys: kinds of ship

tight: sound, seaworthy

And twice as . . . next: this line may well be spoken as an aside to the audience

out-vied: out-bid (a gambling term)

let your father: if your father

but a cavil: merely a trifling objection

If not, to Signor Gremio: Hortensio has not been present at this 'auction' and his absence may indicate some corruption in the text of the play as we have it

gamester: gambler

Set foot under thy table: be kept by your charity

a toy: a ridiculous suggestion

kind: foolishly gullible

faced it with a card of ten: won the match by guile despite having poor resources (a metaphor from card-playing)

supposed Lucentio: a reference to one of Shakespeare's sources, Gascoigne's *Supposes* (1566)

Fathers commonly ... sire: the device which Tranio has started requires him to reverse nature and 'acquire' a 'father' for his impersonated Lucentio

---

Act III Scene 1

Lucentio, disguised as the tutor Cambio, and Hortensio, in the guise of Licio, attempt to woo Bianca as they give their lessons. Lucentio reveals to her his true identity but Bianca does not yet completely trust him. Hortensio has less success and begins to be disenchanted with Bianca.

NOTES AND GLOSSARY:

Enter Lucentio ... Bianca: some editors add the further stage direction that Hortensio is holding Bianca's hand to teach her the fingering of the lute

Have you so soon forgot ... withal?: a reference to II.1

Preposterous: wishing to put first what should be last: the place of music is to refresh the mind *after* work, not before it

while: when

braves: taunts

breeching scholar: a schoolboy in trousers, liable to be whipped

'pointed: appointed (compare Katherina's words in I.1.102–104)

Take you: addressed to Hortensio

the whiles: for the time being

Hic ibat ... celsa senis: (*Latin*) Here ran the Simois, here in the Sigeian land, Here stood the lofty palace of old Priam (Two lines from Ovid's *Heroides*)

Construe: translate

the old pantaloon: this is the description given to Gremio in I.1, although it might refer here to Baptista

the treble jars: the topmost string is out of tune

Spit in the hole: either Lucentio knows nothing of music or, more likely, he is insulting Hortensio. Spitting into the lute would, in fact, damage it. The only instrument which might be tuned that way would be a pipe

presume not . . . despair not: Bianca's reply, which neither encourages nor rejects Lucentio, is typical of the way in which a lady was expected to treat her courtly lover

bass: lowest string

base: ignoble

jars: interrupts conversation

Pedascule: petty scholar

Aeacides . . . grandfather: in order to delude Hortensio Lucentio goes back to explaining the passage from Ovid. This is an appropriate line for him to interpret, because Ajax had another name (Aeacides), as Lucentio has

my master: (a) my instructor, (b) my husband

makes no music in three parts: include no songs for three voices

so formal: so unable to improvise

gamut: the order of the notes in the scale

in a briefer sort: by a quicker method

'A re'; 'B mi'; 'C fa ut'; 'D sol re'; 'E la mi': these are the musical notes

one clef two notes have I: an obscure line

show pity or I die: again the exaggerated plea of the courtly lover

nice: affected, modern

stale: lure, decoy: a metaphor from hawking

Seize thee that list: anyone who wishes may have thee

Act III Scene 2

Baptista, Katherina and their guests await the arrival of Petruchio on his wedding day. Biondello announces that Petruchio is coming, dressed most unsuitably and on a broken-down old horse. This is proved true when Petruchio arrives, but he refuses to change his clothes, and goes off to meet his bride as he is. Tranio and Lucentio confer and plan the elopement of Lucentio and Bianca. Gremio brings them a report of Petruchio's wedding, where the bridegroom behaved very badly. Petruchio and Katherina enter and he insists that they leave for his house immediately, not even staying for their own wedding-feast. Despite Katherina's protests they go, leaving their friends to celebrate without them.

NOTES AND GLOSSARY:

'pointed: appointed

rudesby: rough fellow

spleen: whims

Patience, good Katherine . . . honest: this speech would be more appropriately spoken by Hortensio, Petruchio's friend, and giving the speech to Tranio may indicate some corruption in the text

passing: very

withal: despite that

old news: rare news

breeches: trousers

thrice turned: turned inside out (to conceal wear) three times

candle-cases: good for nothing but to hold the worn-out remains of candles

chapeless: with no proper scabbard

points: laces

hipped: with broken hips

stirrups of no kindred: stirrups which do not match

possessed with the glanders . . . shoulder shotten: Petruchio's horse is terribly diseased, especially with swellings of the legs and mouth. It also has jaundice and a dislocated shoulder!

near-legged before: its forelegs knocking together

half-checked: wrongly fastened

headstall of sheep's leather: bridle of weak leather, easily broken

velure: velvet

pieced with pack-thread: mended with string

caparisoned: clothed

linen stock . . . kersey boot-hose: unmatching stockings

list: strip of cloth

the humour of forty fancies: it is not clear what this reference means

Gentles: gentlemen

methinks: it seems to me

wondrous monument: terrible omen

prodigy: strange occurrence

unprovided: inappropriately dressed

doff this habit: take off these clothes

your estate: your social position

Sufficeth it: let it be sufficient

enforced to digress: obliged to depart from tradition

unreverent: disrespectful

Good sooth: certainly

what she will wear in me: a bawdy allusion to the tiring effect that marriage will have on Petruchio

seal the title . . . kiss: although the audience do not see the wedding, we do witness the 'lovely kiss' in V.1

to love concerneth . . . father's liking: it is necessary to add Baptista's approval to Bianca's love for you

narrowly: carefully

steal our marriage: elope

let all the world say no: even if all the world were to disagree

quaint: skilful

As willingly . . . from school: (a) being as happy to leave as I was to leave school, (b) having learned as much as ever I did at school

groom: rough peasant

curster: more cursed

a fool to him: an innocent creature compared with him

Should ask: asked

by gogs-wouns: by God's wounds—a very inappropriate expression on this occasion

took him such a cuff: gave him such a blow

'Now take . . . any list': Petruchio appears to strike the priest because he believes that the priest was trying to lift up Katherina's skirts. This line is a challenge to anyone else bold enough to attempt this discourtesy: 'Let anyone else try to take up her skirts if he dare'

cozen: cheat

sops: the dregs of the wine

to ask him sops: to need sops (to make it grow better)

Make it no wonder: do not be surprised

the oats have eaten the horses: he means that the horses have eaten the oats

You may be . . . green: be off as soon as you wish

jolly: arrogant

what hast thou to do?: what business is it of yours?

domineer: riot

or go hang yourselves: do what you please

She is my goods . . . my any thing: Petruchio claims possession of Katherina as his property

Fear not, sweet wench: Petruchio pretends that he is rescuing Kate from attackers

buckler thee: protect you with my sword

Went they not: If they had not gone

Kated: (a) afflicted with Kate (as with a disease), (b) pun on 'mated'—mad, amazed

wants: are missing

wants no junkets: no delicacies are missing

bride it: play the bride

Act IV Scene 1

Grumio arrives first at Petruchio's house to warn the other servants to prepare for the coming of Petruchio and Katherina. He tells Curtis, a fellow-servant, of their misadventures on the way home. When the bridal pair enters, Petruchio finds fault with all the servants and refuses to allow Katherina to eat. In a soliloquy Petruchio reveals to the audience that he intends to tame his wife as he would a falcon, depriving her of food and sleep until she submits.

NOTES AND GLOSSARY:

rayed:	dirtied
a little pot and soon hot:	a short man easily angered
so coldly:	so abruptly
fire, fire, cast on no water:	a parody of the chorus of a popular song: 'Fire, fire, cast on water'
I am no beast:	in the previous speech Grumio has compared himself with a beast, and Curtis here refuses to be a fellow to him
thy horn is a foot . . . the least:	a bawdy allusion to their sexual prowess
cold world:	unfriendly world
cony-catching:	evasive answers
rushes:	the usual floor covering
Jacks . . . Jills:	male and female servants
carpets:	table-cloths
fallen out:	(a) in disagreement, (b) fallen from their saddles
sensible:	(a) logical, (b) one that can be 'sensed', felt
Imprimis:	(*Latin*) first
hadst thou not crossed me, thou shouldst have heard:	in fact, of course, Grumio does give all these details to Curtis in the mere act of refusing to give them
bemoiled:	dirtied
By this reckoning . . . than she:	Curtis must know what Petruchio is really like, and so this line can only imply that he realises that Petruchio is acting, pretending to be a shrew
of an indifferent knit:	of a respectable colour
countenance:	(a) greet, (b) face
credit:	(a) do honour to, (b) lend money to
spruce:	smart
Cock's passion:	by God's passion (an oath)
whoreson malt-horse drudge:	cursedly slow creature
all unpinked:	not properly decorated
link:	the blacking used to die hats

Why, when I say?: the humour throughout the rest of the scene comes from Petruchio's complaints about servants who are in fact quite efficient, and food which is properly cooked

you have a stomach: (a) you have an appetite, (b) you are proud

give thanks: say the prayer before the meal

trenchers: plates

engenders choler: leads to anger. The Elizabethans thought that diet had a particularly strong effect on a person's temperament

fast: go without food

of ourselves: by our own nature

for company: together

kills her: defeats her

politicly: deliberately

My falcon ... be obedient: this is an extended metaphor which compares the taming of Katherina with the training of a hunting hawk

sharp and passing empty: famished and very hungry

stoop: is willing to fly to the lure

full-gorged: fully fed

then she never looks upon her love: if she is fed she will be unwilling to return to her trainer

man my haggard: train my wild hawk

watch her: make her stay awake

kites: falcons (a pun on 'Kate': see II.1)

bate and beat: flutter and beat their wings

eat: ate

hurly: chaos

intend: shall pretend

to kill a wife with kindness: an ironic allusion to a proverb. 'To kill a wife with kindness' meant to make a woman disobedient by being too indulgent. Petruchio's plan is quite the reverse

Act IV Scene 2

Hortensio, still disguised as Licio, brings Tranio, also still in disguise, to watch Lucentio wooing Bianca at her lessons. Hortensio reveals his true identity to Tranio and they agree to court Bianca no longer. Hortensio leaves to marry a wealthy widow. Tranio is reporting all this to the lovers when Biondello announces the arrival of an old man whom Tranio deceives. Tranio pretends to be Lucentio and persuades the old man to impersonate Vincentio, Lucentio's father.

NOTES AND GLOSSARY:

fancy:	favour
bears me fair in hand:	encourages me
that I profess:	what I am teaching
The Art to Love:	*Ars Amatoria*, Ovid's text-book of courtly love
master of your art:	a joke based upon the university degree, Master of Arts
heart:	pun on 'art'
proceeders:	a proceeder is a scholar who moves from the degree of BA (Bachelor of Arts) to MA (Master of Arts)
wonderful:	incredible
For:	for the sake of
cullion:	servant
lightness:	(a) fickleness, (b) pun on the meaning of Bianca's name: 'white'
Forswear:	abandon
unfeigned oath:	a nice piece of irony. Tranio is abandoning Bianca, although in reality he has never seriously courted her
haggard:	Petruchio called Katherina a haggard in the previous scene
'longeth to:	is appropriate to
ta'en you napping:	caught you at your wooing
lusty:	pleasant
unto the taming-school:	Hortensio has not told Tranio where he has gone. This seems to be another indication that the roles of Tranio and Hortensio have been revised at some stage
tricks eleven and twenty long:	a great amount of tricks
an ancient angel:	an old man
marcantant:	(*Italian*) merchant
pedant:	schoolmaster. The old man has come to transact business (lines 88–90) and so appears to be a merchant, even though he is labelled 'Pedant' by the stage directions
formal in apparel:	sober in dress
Take in your love:	take Bianca inside
farrer:	further
Tis death for . . . Padua:	this ruse is borrowed from Shakespeare's *The Comedy of Errors*
your ships are stayed:	the ships from your city are kept in custody
as much as an apple doth an oyster:	that is, not at all
friendly:	as a friend
take upon you:	behave

looked for:	expected
pass assurance:	give a guarantee

Act IV Scene 3

In Petruchio's house Katherina pleads in vain for Grumio to give her food. Petruchio and Hortensio enter and Petruchio announces that they are to visit Baptista. He brings in a haberdasher and a tailor with a cap and a gown for Katherina. However, he deliberately finds fault with the new clothes and refuses to let Katherina keep them, even though she wants to. They leave for Padua in their old clothes.

NOTES AND GLOSSARY:

forsooth, I dare not:	in truth, I dare not. Grumio is refusing to give food to Katherina
a present alms:	an immediate gift of charity
As who to say:	as if to say
neat's foot:	calf's foot
passing good:	very good
too choleric a meat:	see the note on 'engenders choler' in IV.1 above
let the mustard rest:	leave out the mustard
the very name:	the name alone
amort:	melancholy
What cheer?:	how are things with you?
dress:	prepare
sorted to no proof:	come to nothing
apace:	quickly
as bravely:	as well dressed
ruffs:	fashionable starched collars
farthingales:	hooped skirts
bravery:	clothing
ruffling treasure:	treasure full of ruffs
bespeak:	order to be made
moulded on a porringer:	shaped like a porridge dish
doth fit the time:	is fashionable
custard-coffin:	crust of a custard-pie
masquing stuff:	clothes suitable only to be worn as a costume in a masque (a courtly dramatic entertainment involving dancing and disguise)
a demi-cannon:	a large cannon
a censer:	an incense-burner
a devil's name:	in the devil's name
like to:	likely to
Marry, and did:	certainly I did

mar it to the time: spoil it for all time
hop me: the 'me' is redundant; see note on 'knock me here' in I.2
kennel: gutter
quaint: intricate
Belike: perhaps
puppet: fool
he means: that is, the tailor
nail: one-sixteenth of a yard
nit: louse's egg
Braved: defied
bemete: (a) measure, (b) beat
think on prating while thou liv'st: remember to avoid idle chatter for the rest of your life
Faced: trimmed
Face: defy
braved: clothed
brave: challenge
Ergo: (*Latin*) therefore
lies in's throat: is entirely untrue
Imprimis: (*Latin*) first
bottom: spool
bill: (a) the note which the tailor is reading, (b) indictment, accusation
prove upon thee: that is, by fighting a duel
an I had thee in place where: If I had you in an appropriate place
mete-yard: measuring-stick
God-a-mercy: God have mercy
have no odds: have no chance. Grumio has armed himself with a measuring-stick, giving the tailor a piece of paper to fight him with
take it up unto: take it away for
Take up my mistress' gown: Grumio interprets Petruchio's order as a command to undress Katherina
habiliments: clothes
peereth: (a) peep through, (b) appears
habit: suit of clothes
furniture: clothing
frolic: be glad
to him: that is, to Baptista
dinner-time: midday
supper-time: about six pm
this gallant will command the sun: Hortensio unwittingly anticipates Petruchio's actual words in IV.5

Act IV Scene 4

Tranio, still impersonating his master, and the pedant, as Vincentio, meet Baptista and agree on a marriage contract between Tranio and Bianca. The real Lucentio watches all this and plans with Biondello his elopement with Bianca.

NOTES AND GLOSSARY:

but I be:	unless I am
Pegasus:	a common name for an English inn
'longeth to:	is appropriate to
schooled:	trained to play his part properly
a tall fellow, hold thee that to drink:	a capable fellow, take this to buy yourself a drink
stay:	hinder
matched:	married
curious:	niggling
or both dissemble:	a nice piece of irony: Tranio and Bianca are dissembling, that is, pretending, and have no love for each other
pass:	settle in law
affied:	betrothed
Pitchers have ears:	a proverbial allusion to the possibility of servants overhearing their arrangements, again ironic since Tranio is himself a servant
happily:	perhaps
an it like you:	if that pleases you
scrivener:	officer authorised to draw up legal contracts
pittance:	food
one mess:	a single dish
What say'st thou Biondello?:	the editors of the New Cambridge edition of the play claim that the rest of this scene is not by Shakespeare, because Biondello speaks impertinently to Lucentio. However, it could be argued that this impertinence is consistent with Biondello's character
'has:	he has
counterfeit:	pretended (a metaphor from printing)
cum privilegio ad imprimendum solum:	(*Latin*) another printing metaphor. This phrase was frequently printed on the title pages of books and means 'with the sole right of printing'
your appendix:	that is, Bianca (another printing metaphor; an appendix is a supplement printed at the end of a book)

then wherefore should I doubt?: this may indicate that Lucentio already has doubts about the obedience of his future wife
Hap what hap may, I'll roundly go about her: Whatever happens, I'll approach her frankly

---

Act IV Scene 5

As Petruchio, Katherina and Hortensio are travelling back to Padua, Petruchio is able to persuade his wife to agree with him that it is night, even though it is in reality daytime. She is persuaded to greet an old man they meet as if he were a beautiful young girl. The old man is discovered to be Vincentio, Lucentio's father, and Petruchio and Katherina apologise to him and they journey on the Padua together. Hortensio feels that he has learned from Petruchio how to treat a wife.

NOTES AND GLOSSARY:
a God's name: in God's name
what I list: what I please
Or e'er I: before I will ever
crossed: argued with
a rush-candle: a feeble kind of candle
go thy ways, the field is won: carry on, you have won the battle
Thus the bowl . . . the bias: this is the way things should be, to exploit the natural tendencies of others to get what you want. The game of bowls is played with balls which have a weight on one side, and the skill of the game is to use this weight or 'bias'
'A will: he will
Whither away: where are you going
Happy the parents . . . bedfellow: the parents of such a lovely child are fortunate, as will be the man who is lucky enough to marry you
reverend father: respectable old gentleman
father: here, father-in-law
so qualified as may beseem: having such qualities as are appropriate
jealous: here, suspicious
Have to: now for
untoward: ill-mannered

Act V Scene 1

As the real Lucentio goes off to marry Bianca in secret, his father arrives at Lucentio's house and is denied entry by the pedant, who is impersonating him. Biondello and Tranio deny they know Vincentio and he is

about to be taken off to prison when Bianca and Lucentio arrive.
Lucentio explains the deceit to Baptista and Vincentio and asks for
their forgiveness. Katherina and Petruchio have witnessed all of this
confusion and they seal their own marriage with a kiss.

NOTES AND GLOSSARY:

Gremio is out before: Gremio is at the front of the stage and the opening
lines are spoken behind his back

the church o' your back: the church ceremony completed, and you outside the church

My father's: Baptista's house

some cheer is toward: some refreshment is likely

what he that knocks: this part of the scene, in which Vincentio is denied
entry to his son's house, is very similar to Shake-
speare's *The Comedy of Errors*, III.1

from Mantua: the pedant has forgotten which city he is supposed
to have come from

Why, how now, gentlemen!: Petruchio adds to the comedy of this scene
by assuming that it is Vincentio who is lying

'a means to cozen: he intends to defraud

under my countenance: using my identity

crack-hemp: someone wicked enough to be hanged

I hope I may choose, sir: I'll come if I so choose. Biondello denies that
Vincentio has a right to give him orders

a copatain hat: tall, pointed hat

good husband: careful manager

your habit: your clothing

what 'cerns it you: what business is it of yours

maintain it: afford it

Bergamo: the traditional home of the servant character in
Italian comedy

be forthcoming: appears to answer charges against him at his trial

cony-catched: deceived

yonder he is: the 'he' is Vincentio

counterfeit supposes: false pretences. An illusion to Gascoigne's *Supposes*. Compare note on 'supposed Lucentio', II.1

eyne: eyes

packing, with a witness: deceit, certainly

faced and braved: defied and challenged

go to: do not worry

My cake is dough: my hopes are failed. Compare Gremio's speech, I.1

Out of hope of all but: hoping for nothing but

Act V Scene 2

At the feast to celebrate the wedding of Bianca and Lucentio, there is joking between the wives (including Hortensio's new bride) over Katherina's previous shrewish behaviour. When the men are left alone, Petruchio proposes a wager, whereby each man sends a servant to fetch his wife, to determine which of the three is the most obedient. Bianca and Hortensio's wife refuse to come, but Katherina answers her husband's call and, having brought in the other two wives, delivers them a lecture on the duties a wife owes her husband.

NOTES AND GLOSSARY:

At last, though long: at long last

jarring notes: discord (possibly a reference to Hortensio's posing as a music teacher)

scapes: escapes

close out stomachs up: settle our differences

fears: is afraid of

afeared: frightened

He that is giddy . . . round: a man in trouble imagines everyone else is at fault

Thus I conceive by him: I mean this to apply to him

my office: my job. It is Hortensio's role to make his wife submissive

An hasty-witted body: a quick-witted person

bird: prey

Lucentio slipped me . . . .for his master: Lucentio employed me as a man unleashes his greyhound, to run and hunt on his behalf

currish: (a) vulgar, (b) like a dog

deer: a pun on 'dear', beloved

hold you at a bay: a deer is 'at bay' when it defends itself against the hounds

gird: taunt

as the jest did . . . outright: as the joke bounced off me I am certain it harmed you two thoroughly

in good sadness: seriously

I'll venture so much of my hawk or hound: I would risk as much on a wager about my hawk or hound

I'll be your half: I'll pay half your stake money

by my holidame: by my holy lady (an oath)

Swinge me them: the 'me' is redundant

An awful rule: a rule based upon respect

what not: everything

Another dowry . . . daughter: Katherina is so altered that Baptista offers a secondary dowry for her

bite the meads: attack the meadows

meet or amiable: appropriate or desirable

moved: angered

watch: stay awake on duty

craves: desires

fair looks: looks of love

simple: foolish

unable worms: weak creatures

reason: intelligence

vail your stomachs, for it is no boot: cast off your pride for it will gain you nothing

go thy ways . . . ha't: well done, you have won the prize

sped: defeated

white: a pun on the meaning of Bianca's name

Part 3

Commentary

Date and sources

Shakespeare's plays can be dated by the following means: some plays were published during his lifetime and, clearly, must have been written before the date of their publication; other plays contain allusions to contemporary events or phenomena, which help us to establish the date of composition; some of the plays were listed by Francis Meres in 1598 and must therefore have been written before that time; for others we have recorded dates of performances; finally, in the absence of other evidence, it is possible to group certain plays together on the grounds of similarities in either style or theme and thus establish a relative set of dates.

It is more difficult to date *The Taming of the Shrew* than many of Shakespeare's other works. Meres lists the following works in *Palladis Tamia*:

> For comedy, witness his *Gentlemen of Verona*, his *Errors*, his *Love Labours lost*, his *Love Labours wonne*, his *Midsummer night's dreame*, and his *Merchant of Venice*.

There is no reference here to *The Taming of the Shrew* (unless that is the play which Meres calls *Love labours wonne*), and yet most critics feel that this had been written well before 1598.

The question of the date of publication of *The Taming of the Shrew* is complicated by the fact that a different play entitled *The Taming of a Shrew* was published in 1594 and performed regularly in the late sixteenth century. Even when Samuel Pepys refers as late as 1667 to a performance of a play which he did not like called 'A Shrew', it is clear that it was not Shakespeare's play which he had seen but some other version.

The Taming of a Shrew may be an alternative version of the play written by Shakespeare; it may be an older play which Shakespeare used as his source; or it may be a pirated version of Shakespeare's play reconstructed from memory by someone who had either acted in or seen Shakespeare's comedy. The three plots are common to both plays: both have an Induction, the story of the taming of a shrewish girl, and the less troubled courtship of another sister. However, names of the characters in *The Taming of a Shrew* are almost all different; the shrew is given two sisters; and there is a closing scene involving Christopher Sly. The opinion of most current scholars is that *The Taming of a Shrew* is a reconstructed version of Shakespeare's play and that, therefore, *The Taming of the Shrew* must have been written before 1594.*

This relatively early date is supported by the style of the play and by its relationship with another early comedy, *The Comedy of Errors*. In many respects *The Taming of the Shrew* is less sophisticated than other Shakespearean comedies. Its humour arises more often from farcical situations and from visual spectacle than from verbal witticism. The relationship between Grumio and Petruchio, for example, is amusing because Grumio lives in continual threat of being beaten, and we laugh at his physical predicament. Although Petruchio does not need to use violence to tame Kate, there is no doubt of his capacity for violence, and this keeps the main tone of this part of the play close to that of farce. Katherina beats Hortensio and Bianca, asserting her own violent nature and her physical power: Petruchio finally subdues her to the extent that she will place her hand under his foot. The play includes considerable physical humour which does not require the support of sophisticated dialogue for the audience to find it amusing.

In this respect it resembles *The Comedy of Errors* where we also find masters and mistresses becoming infuriated and beating their servants in their anger; again, the frenzied activity of the actors and the ridiculousness of the situations in which they find themselves make a major contribution to the success of the play. The two plays also share a rather mechanical device for setting the play in motion: in both a character is required to recapitulate, for the audience's benefit, the story of what has happened to him before the play began. In *The Comedy of Errors* it is Aegeon who recounts his incredible tale of misfortunes and coincidences. In *The Taming of the Shrew*, Lucentio is required to explain his background and his reasons for being in Padua.

The two plays even share common incidents: Aegeon in *The Comedy of Errors* is under sentence of death because of a dispute between two trading cities, Ephesus and Syracuse, just such a dispute as Tranio alleges to exist between Mantua and Padua in *The Taming of the Shrew* (IV.2). Vincentio, in *The Taming of the Shrew* (V.1), is denied entry to his son's house while an impostor eats within, just as Antipholus of Ephesus in *The Comedy of Errors* is denied entry to his house while his twin brother is entertained in his place.

Finally, the two plays are linked in that *The Comedy of Errors* touches on what is to be a major theme in *The Taming of the Shrew*: the topic of

*The scholarship on this controversy is fully dealt with by Richard Hosley in 'Sources and Analogues of *The Taming of the Shrew*', reprinted in William Shakespeare, *The Taming of the Shrew*, ed. R.B. Heilman, The Signet Classic Shakespeare, New American Library, London, 1966, pp.186–208.

who should be the dominant partner in marriage. Adriana i
Comedy of Errors looks like a model for the true shrew Katherina

The Taming of the Shrew contains three elements in its plot-structure:
the Christopher Sly scenes, the wooing of Bianca, and the taming of
Katherina. The Sly scenes are an example of a very common fairy-tale
in which a beggar is turned into a prince while he sleeps. The story
occurs, for example, in *The Arabian Nights* where the trickster is
Haroun Al Raschid. The story of the wooing of Bianca seems to have
been borrowed by Shakespeare from George Gascoigne's play *Supposes*, which in turn derives from the Italian comedy *I Suppositi* by
Ariosto (1474-1533), an Italian comic writer. Shakespeare's play draws
attention to its source by emphasising the very word 'supposed' (II.1
and V.1). Furthermore Gascoigne's play has a number of suitors vying
for the hand of a single heroine; it has an Italian setting; it includes a
character called Petrucio, and a father who is most interested in securing
as large a dowry as possible for his daughter. However, a significant
difference between *Supposes* and the Bianca plot is that in the former the
heroine is already pregnant by her lover. Shakespeare's heroine, in a
manner typical of his comedies, remains chaste until her wedding.

The third element in the plot structure of the play, the taming of a
shrewish wife, was a common motif in English literature, especially in
the folk ballads. One such ballad is the anonymous *Merry Jest of a
Shrewde and Curste Wife* (1550), in which the husband's behaviour is
so extreme as to make Petruchio appear lenient in comparison. In the
ballad the husband whips his wife and wraps her exhausted body in the
skin of an old horse which he has salted to make her wounds even more
painful. Petruchio succeeds with rather more humane techniques.

A play for actors

One of Shakespeare's favourite devices is to remind his audience that
they are watching a play. Sometimes he does this by having his characters compare life to a play:

All the world's a stage
And all the men and women merely players.
(*As You Like It*, II.7.139-40)

Sometimes his characters sit down and watch as other actors perform
a play for their entertainment: this happens in *Hamlet*, *A Midsummer
Night's Dream*, and *Love's Labour's Lost*. Nowhere is this device more
fully exploited than in *The Taming of the Shrew*. We are continually
reminded that we are watching actors performing roles which are not
real and which they will perform only for a brief period of time before
returning to normality once again.

From the very start of the play we see characters playing out roles which are unnatural to them. Sly is forced into the role of a lord (a part he is at first reluctant to accept) while the real lord acts out the part of a servant and provides Sly with a false 'wife'. It is into this situation that the actors enter who are to perform the main action of the play, who are to act the parts of Bianca, Katherina, Petruchio and the rest. They appear in the Induction as players, and we are therefore aware at the outset that the story of Bianca and Katherina is an unreal show. Furthermore, this show is acted under false pretences, for the players think that they are performing it for an eccentric lord, not a drunken tinker.

Thus, as the main action of the play begins, we have characters coming on to the stage to play the roles of Lucentio and Tranio while on the balcony above them sits the 'audience' of Sly, the lord and the page. The real audience in the theatre would appreciate that characters on the upper level of the stage were generally superior in status to those below (much is made of this, for example, in Shakespeare's *Richard II*), but there is added humour here in that although the actors believe that they are watched by a lord and his court, the only member of this 'audience' who is a gentleman is disguised as a servant.

The play which is performed in the house of this English nobleman is itself set in Italy and the travelling players who act it are very close indeed to the professional Italian *commedia dell' arte* school. They include in their number two of the standard figures from this tradition: an old 'pantaloon' (Gremio) and a clever servant (Tranio), who comes from Bergamo, the home of Harlequin, the servant in the *commedia dell' arte*.

However, we are never allowed to believe that they are really Italian, for they continually assert their English characteristics. Grumio does not know the difference between Italian and Latin (I.2); the pedant talks of English taverns he has stayed in (IV.4); and the oaths which Petruchio uses are all English curses. They are English actors pretending to be Italian, and we are not allowed to forget this.

These actors are allowed to demonstrate their versatility and skill in the main plot. The player who acts the part of Tranio has to represent a servant acting the part of a gentleman, and a good deal of the humour of such lines as these comes from our awareness that Tranio is only pretending to be a gentleman:

Softly, my masters! If you be gentlemen
Do me this right—hear me with patience. (I.2.237–8)

Tranio frequently accuses others of ungentlemanly conduct.

He is not the only servant allowed to act another role. When he first impersonates Lucentio he is ably supported by Biondello:

TRANIO: Gentlemen, God save you. If I may be bold,
              Tell me, I beseech you, which is the readi'st way
              To the house of Signor Baptista Minola?
BIONDELLO: He that has the two fair daughters—is't he you mean?
TRANIO: Even he, Biondello.
                          (I.2.216–21)

This exchange has all the signs of having been carefully rehearsed by the two servants to give more substance to Tranio's pretence. At the end of that same scene Tranio convinces Gremio and Hortensio that he is their equal, and Grumio and Biondello demonstrate that they too can talk like gentlemen as they say:

O excellent motion! Fellows, let's be gone. (I.2.277)

The play, especially in the Bianca plot, is full of disguises and impersonations, as well as of characters watching the activities of others, and becoming an audience to that activity. For example, in Act IV Scene 2, Tranio (a servant impersonating his master) and Hortensio (a gentleman disguised as a servant) watch as Lucentio (a gentleman disguised as a servant) woos Bianca. Tranio and Hortensio constitute an audience watching Bianca and Lucentio while they are watched in turn by Sly and his 'court', which in its turn is being watched by the audience in the theatre. A particular irony in this scene is that Hortensio, although he is himself disguised, assumes that the other characters are what they appear to be: that Tranio is a gentleman and that Lucentio is merely a tutor.

In contrast to both the Bianca plot and the Induction, that part of the play which is concerned with the taming of Katherina seems to involve no complex disguises or impersonations. However, it is in this part of the play that we are most aware that we are not watching something real, for Petruchio is continually putting on an act and pretending to be what he is not. One of the strengths of *The Taming of the Shrew* is that Shakespeare weaves together three separate stories into a single unified whole. There are characters in each of these three stories who assume disguises or false personalities and this is one way in which the unity of the play is maintained. Petruchio does not change places with his servant or adopt an assumed name, but in other, more subtle ways he frequently reminds us that he is an actor.

The characters

Critics of *The Taming of the Shrew* express widely different reactions to the play. Shaw found it 'disgusting to modern sensibility', objecting to the crudeness of its farce and finding no sympathy for Katherina, who binds and beats her sister, or for Petruchio, who starves and humiliates his wife.* Quiller-Couch also expressed some unease about the play and almost apologises for it:

> The trouble about *The Shrew* is that, although it reads rather ill in the library, it goes very well on the stage. Being a play which invites rant and in places even demands it, *The Shrew* as naturally tempts the impersonator to unintelligible shouting and mouthing. Yet there is a delicacy in the man underlying his boisterousness.*

More recent critics have interpreted the play with more gravity than it deserves by attempting to find valid psychological grounds for the actions of both Katherina (whom they see as being harshly treated by her father) and Petruchio.† It is not necessary to go to such lengths. It is possible to arrive at an interpretation of the play which admits its farcical nature without being driven to despise either Petruchio or Katherina, so long as one remembers that Petruchio is an 'impersonator'.

We first encounter Petruchio in Act I Scene 2, and he forms an immediate and marked contrast with the other new arrival in Padua, Lucentio, whom we saw in the preceding scene. Petruchio's reasons for coming to Padua are clear: he has come to find a wife, and he pursues that aim consistently. Lucentio apparently came to study, but is soon led astray from his intention and diverted into courting Bianca. Petruchio treats his servant roughly and impatiently: there is none of the casual good humour that exists between Lucentio and Tranio, and our first impression of Petruchio is probably that he is less attractive and more violent than Lucentio.

The contrast between Petruchio and Lucentio as they begin their wooing is very marked. Petruchio has been an adventurer, a traveller who has experienced a range of mishaps and troubles:

> Have I not in my time heard lions roar?
> Have I not heard the sea, puffed up with winds,
> Rage like an angry boar chafed with sweat?
> Have I not heard great ordnance in the field,
> And heaven's artillery thunder in the skies?
> (I.2.198–201)

He has arrived by sea, blown by the 'happy gale' of fortune, and he plans to 'board' Katherina as one would take possession of a ship. Lucentio,

---

* *Saturday Review*, 6 November 1897.
* *The Taming of the Shrew*, edited by Sir A. Quiller-Couch and J. Dover Wilson, Cambridge University Press, London, 1928, p.xxv.
* See, for example, Nevill Coghill, 'The Basis of Shakespearean Comedy', in *The Taming of the Shrew*, ed. R.B. Heilman, The Signet Classic Shakespeare, New American Library, London, 1966, pp.167–9.

on the other hand, has led a much less exciting life at home in Pisa and is much more idealistic than Petruchio.

Petruchio makes no pretence of being in love; he has decided to marry Katherina before he has even seen her, attracted by her wealth alone. He has no rivals in his wooing and is allowed free access to her. However, Petruchio is presented with a challenge, that of changing Kate from an unacceptable shrew into a reasonable wife with whom he can live happily. The wooers of Bianca assume that no change is either necessary or likely in her case, but they are deluding themselves.

Petruchio has few allusions about the task he is embarking upon, nor of his likely success:

> As wealth is burden of my wooing dance—
> Be she as foul as was Florentius' love . . .
> She moves me not.
> (I.2.67–72)

He is marrying for money but he is also well aware that men like Florentius have married apparently unattractive wives only to find them later to be beautiful in every respect.

Petruchio's strategy in winning Katherina is simple: he will pretend to be more perverse than she is and will act as if everything were the opposite of what it really is. Thus he will convince her of her own folly by exaggerating her own faults in his performance. Grumio knows his master and has faith in Petruchio's ability to act the part:

> She may perhaps call him half a score knaves or so. Why, that's nothing; an he begin once, he'll rail in his rope-tricks. I'll tell you what, sir, an she stand him but a little, he will throw a figure in her face, and so disfigure her with it that she shall have no more eyes to see withal than a cat. You know him not, sir.
> (I.2.108–114)

This speech is significant in a number of ways. Firstly, it implies in its final sentence that Petruchio is capable of behaviour which will surprise even his close friend Hortensio. Secondly, it emphasises that Petruchio's method of mastering Katherina is likely to be through words rather than physical brutality. Grumio is slightly misleading here for he suggests that Petruchio will use rhetoric ('rope-tricks' as he calls it), the skilful use of language to persuade others. Petruchio, in fact, hardly tries to persuade Katherina at all; he simply makes assertions. She has either to accept them or suffer the consequences.

This is not to suggest that Petruchio has no rhetorical skill, or that this skill is not in evidence very early in the play. At the opening of the second act the audience should be keen with anticipation. We have met both Katherina and Petruchio, seen her waywardness and heard his determination to win her. As yet, however, they have not met and the audience will be eagerly awaiting this first encounter. Petruchio's first words in the second act show the tactic he is to employ, and the way in which this strategy is to depend upon language and rhetoric. He tells the astonished Baptista that he has heard of Katherina:

> . . . of her beauty and her wit,
> Her affability and bashful modesty,
> Her wondrous qualities and mild behaviour
> (II.1.48–50)

Thus Petruchio embarks on his conquest by simply pretending to believe that everything is the exact opposite of what he knows it to be. He is intent on enjoying himself and treats the whole venture as if he were attending a play:

> . . . for an entrance to my entertainment
> I do present you with a man of mine.
> (II.1.54–5)

When he is left alone, Petruchio makes it clear to the audience that he intends to continue acting in this perverse fashion:

> Say that she rail, why then I'll tell her plain
> She sings as sweetly as a nightingale.
> (II.1.170–1)

and in an extraordinarily unromantic first meeting with Katherina, he simply ignores all her protests and asserts that he will have his will. He intends to change her from a wild-cat to a domestic cat, to a cake, a delicacy to be enjoyed and savoured. In these puns on Katherina's name Petruchio displays his facility with words, but he is not using rhetoric to persuade her, merely to assert what will inevitably happen. Their conversation does not appear to have led very far, yet Petruchio is unabashed; he dismisses all that has been said as trivial ('setting all this chat aside') and, when Baptista re-enters, Petruchio claims a victory that in reality is far from being his. As he claims Kate is mild:

> She's not froward, but modest as the dove
> She is not hot, but temperate as the morn.
> (II.1.286–7)

she makes it clear that this is not the truth. Finally the reality of her behaviour becomes too evident even for Petruchio's acting ability and he is driven to another ruse: he claims that they have arranged that she 'shall still be curst in company' although in private she has been tamed.

Baptista's reaction to Petruchio's extravagant behaviour is worth close attention.

He is very worried about letting his daughter marry after such an odd courtship, and is even more startled when Petruchio arrives in such fantastic garb for the wedding. Baptista has more reason to fear the deceits of Lucentio and Tranio if he did but realise it, yet he trusts to their apparent honesty. Petruchio, of course, refuses to acknowledge that his clothes are inappropriate and even hints that there is a reason for the way he has dressed (although nobody understands him):

> I am come to keep my word,
> Though in some part enforced to digress,
> Which at more leisure I will so excuse
> As you shall well be satisfied withal.
>   (II.2.105–8)

Petruchio gives a similar hint when he decides to leave with Katherina before the wedding feast:

> If you knew my business,
> You would entreat me rather go than stay
>   (III.2.190–1)

Throughout Act IV Petruchio maintains his act of saying that things are the opposite of what they are, in order to persuade Katherina out of her perversity (as he makes clear in his soliloquy at the end of Act IV Scene 1). An excellent example of this technique occurs in Act IV Scene 3, when Petruchio not only rejects the handiwork of the haberdasher and the tailor (even though the hat and the dress are perfectly well made) but pretends to misunderstand Katherina's objection:

> KATHERINA: . . . I never saw a better-fashioned gown . . .
>   Belike you mean to make a puppet of me.
> PETRUCHIO: Why, true, he means to make a puppet of thee
> TAILOR: She says your worship means to make a puppet of her.
> PETRUCHIO: O monstrous arrogance!
>   (IV.3.101–6)

Petruchio then goes on to abuse the tailor in the most appropriate language, using images from tailoring ('thou rag, thou quantity, thou remnant').

After all his perversity and pretence Petruchio finally discovers whether his tactic has worked, whether Katherina has been tamed, in Act IV Scene 5, as they travel back to Padua. The actress who plays Katherina is given considerable scope in this scene to indicate how willingly she submits to Petruchio's domination, but she does submit and agree that day is night and that old Vincentio is a beautiful young woman. Petruchio has been successful: he and Katherina seal their marriage publicly with a kiss at the end of Act V Scene 1, and, in the final scene, Katherina demonstrates her reformation by lecturing the other brides on the duty which they owe to their husbands.

It is possible, therefore, to regard Petruchio not as a cruel husband who behaves barbarously towards his wife, but as a highly competent actor who plays out the role of being 'more shrew than she', a role which he will not need to maintain for very long. It is ironic that the whole of the main action of the play serves to prevent Sly from taking his 'wife' to bed and that Petruchio's performance as a shrew-tamer also keeps Katherina and himself from their bed. We should not forget that Petruchio himself has to go without sleep and food as he masters Katherina. Indeed the play is full of references to characters who are forced to stay awake, from Petruchio (who swears in Act 1 Scene 2 that he will not sleep till he sees Katherina) to Biondello (who is 'dog-weary' in Act IV Scene 2). It is finally demonstrated that it is easier for a man to go without sleep than it is for a woman. As Katherina says, it is part of the expected role of a husband who:

> commits his body
> To painful labour both by sea and land,
> To watch the night in storms, the day in cold,
> Whilst thou liest warm at home.
> (V.2.147–50)

It is therefore quite appropriate that Petruchio's last words to his wife should be 'Come Kate, we'll to bed'!

We are concerned throughout the play with characters assuming new roles for a brief period of time before returning to normality again. In the Induction Sly is elevated to the status of a lord, but we know that this is a temporary role. *The Taming of a Shrew* actually ends with Sly being thrust out of the house to resume his life as a tinker, and this final scene is sometimes included in performances of Shakespeare's play too.

In the Bianca plot also, Tranio comments rather ruefully on the temporary freedom which he has been granted:

> Lucentio slipped me like his greyhound, which runs himself, and catches for his master
> (V.2.52–3)

Tranio has been let free for a brief while, but only with the agreement of his master. This image, in which Tranio compares himself to an animal controlled by his master, recalls both the image which Petruchio used to describe his mastery of Katherina:

> Another way I have to man my haggard
> To make her come and know her keeper's call
> (IV.1.179–80)

and the fact that the play opens with a lord who controls his servants as he controls his hounds. We should be unfair to Petruchio if we did not realise that he is not the only character to treat people as if they were animals. In the final scene all the men agree willingly to wager money on the obedience of their wives, just as someone might wager on a greyhound.

Marriage, money and social status

The main theme of the play is marriage, and we are given four examples of marriage and courtship to compare: Sly and his 'wife'; Bianca and her suitors; Petruchio and Katherina; and Hortensio and the widow. Through these examples we are shown a range of possible relationships between men and women.

The first and last speeches on the duties of a wife are rather similar. Sly's 'wife' is as obedient as his servants:

My husband and my lord, my lord and husband,
I am your wife in all obedience
(Induction, 2.105-6)

and this is the role that Katherina advocates in the final scene as she lectures the other wives:

Thy husband is thy lord, the life, thy keeper,
Thy head, thy sovereign.
(V.2.145-6)

You might feel that, because these views were first expressed by a character who is merely playing a part (the page Bartholomew pretending to be Sly's wife), you should not take Katherina's final speech as her sincere opinion. However, this last speech of some fifty lines is too long to be sustained as a piece of irony and must be taken at its face value. Furthermore, the portrayal of a wife as inferior to her husband, obedient to him as a servant to his master, is closer to the reality of marriage in Elizabethan England. Neither Katherina, Bianca nor Hortensio's wife is expected to be anything other than servile after marriage, however they may have been treated during their courtship. It is possible, therefore, to see the earlier behaviour of Katherina and Bianca as attempts to make the most of their independence before marriage, knowing how little power they will have afterwards.

In *The Comedy of Errors* Shakespeare had advanced the notion that 'a man is master of his liberty' and that a woman's duty was to 'practise to obey', to be like a servant who has little choice or control over his life. A very similar picture of a woman's lot is painted in *The Taming of the Shrew*. The fates of Katherina and Bianca lie in the hands of th...

father, Baptista. They live under his orders before their marriages and the choice of suitable husbands for them is entirely his.

Marriage in this play is very intimately connected with money and trade. We probably remember most clearly Petruchio's frank avowal that he has come to 'wive it wealthily' but we should not forget that all of the central male characters are involved in one way or another in the financial aspects of marriage. The three suitors of Bianca are willing to pay Petruchio's expenses in wooing Katherina; Gremio pays Lucentio to woo on his behalf; Hortensio refers to Bianca as 'my treasure', and Baptista is anxious to profit from the marriage of his daughters.

Katherina's first words state her objections to being treated as a piece of property:

I pray you, sir, is it your will
To make a stale of me amongst these mates?
(I.1.59-60)

She is unwilling to be sold as if she were a prostitute. The fact is, of course, that Katherina avoids being auctioned in this way by appearing so difficult and unattractive. It may be for this very reason that she behaves so shrewishly: it is her way of asserting her independence.

Baptista is unable to find many potential buyers for Katherina and, although he displays some fatherly care in insisting that Petruchio obtains her love:

When the special thing is well obtained,
That is her love; for that is all in all
(II.1.128-9)

he is still willing to pay a dowry to rid himself of Katherina, however oddly Petruchio might behave.

In contrast, Baptista is able to make a very different financial agreement for his other daughter. Bianca appears a more marketable proposition, and, at the end of Act II Scene 1, Baptista is able to accept bids from Grumio and Tranio. This could appear a sordid and unpleasant scene but Shakespeare keeps it comic by having Baptista's plans frustrated. He foolishly accepts the false bid of Tranio and looks forward to a prosperous marriage while, all the time, Bianca is planning her own form of rebellion in marrying Lucentio in secret. Thus Shakespeare reminds us that marriage was partly a commercial transaction, without allowing either of his principal female characters to be actually auctioned.

The suitors in the play, although superficially different, share very similar views on the role of wives in marriage. While the play is concerned with investigating the difference between social classes by having servants temporarily acting as masters, it is concerned also with the connection between marriage and social class. Petruchio's father is known by Baptista and the reputation of Vincentio has also reached Padua: they are, therefore, socially appropriate partners for Katherina and Bianca, because all four are of the same social status.

However, it is not uncommon even today for a suitor to treat his lady as if she were not only equal to him, but his social superior, his queen. Thus Bianca, who objects to being tied like a slave by her sister (II.1), is wooed by Hortensio and Lucentio as if she had power over them: '. . . show pity or I die' (III.1.75–6).

Shakespeare makes the two scenes involving Hortensio, Lucentio and Bianca even more amusing by having the two suitors disguised as tutors and thus further complicating their social relationship with Bianca. They are in the employ of Bianca's father and therefore, in a sense, her servants; but as her teachers, they are in a position of intellectual superiority and become, in a different sense, her masters. Hence the ambiguity of Bianca's remark to Lucentio:

I must believe, my master, else, I promise you,
I should be arguing still upon that doubt
(III.1.52–3)

Although Hortensio and Lucentio woo Bianca as if she were their lady, they do not expect her to be dominant after marriage. Hortensio abandons Bianca because he believes that she has no sense of her social position:

Yet if thy thoughts, Bianca, be so humble
To cast thy wandering eyes on every stale,
Seize thee that list.
(III.1.87–9)

Hortensio feels offended that Bianca should prefer someone who appears to be a tutor, not realising that he himself appears to be a tutor also at this point. Significantly also, he uses here an image from hawking (Bianca is misled like a hawk who flies to a false 'stale'), and this comparison between Bianca and a hawk is developed later in the play.

Of all the characters in the play who are forced to adopt a role, Hortensio is, perhaps, the least convincing. He finds it very difficult to pretend he is anything other than a gentleman and even calls Lucentio 'sirrah' (III.1.15), the term of address usually employed by gentlemen addressing their servants.

Lucentio woos Bianca and wins her, but then discovers that she is not the conventionally obedient wife he had hoped for. In *The Taming of a Shrew* the transformation of Bianca from a modest girl into a shrewish wife is sudden and unexpected. In Shakespeare's play the change is much more subtle.

Bianca gradually takes over the characteristics of Katherina, becoming more wayward as Katherina becomes more obedient. The shift begins as early as Act III Scene 1, when Bianca tells her tutors:

I am no breeching scholar in the schools,
I'll not be tied to hours nor 'pointed times
(III.1.18–19)

This speech recalls the very words used by Katherina in Act I Scene 1 (lines 103–4), and it begins to look as if Bianca, too, might have the potential for being obstinate. She is specifically directed to replace her sister at the end of Act III Scene 2, when Petruchio and Katherina leave before the wedding feast. Baptista wishes the celebration to continue and says:

Lucentio, you shall supply the bridegroom's place
And let Bianca take her sister's room
(III.2.248–9)

The comparison between the two sisters is extended further in Act IV when Petruchio refers to Katherina as a 'haggard' (IV.1.179) and this same word is applied by Hortensio to Bianca in the next scene (IV.2.39).

By the end of Act IV even Lucentio himself seems to feel uncertain of Bianca's behaviour. As he prepares to elope with her he tells the audience:

I may and will, if she be so contented.
She will be pleased, then wherefore should I doubt?
(IV.4.101–2)

But Lucentio is given proof that he had every reason to doubt when his new bride refuses to come at his call. When she is eventually brought by Katherina Bianca is unrepentant; when Lucentio points out that she has lost him his wager her reply is brief and to the point:

The more fool you for laying on my duty.
(V.2.128)

Moral and imagery

The characters in the play learn a lesson as it draws to a close. Baptista learns that his opinion of his daughters has been false: Katherina is obedient and Bianca 'froward'. He also realises that he has been mistaken in his reactions to Tranio, Lucentio, and Petruchio. In their turn Hortensio and Lucentio discover that they may have misjudged Katherina, and that their new brides are very different from what they at first appeared. In the course of the play we see a number of characters quite deliberately obscuring their real selves by borrowing the clothe of others and there is a general preoccupation with clothing and outward appearances. Ultimately, however, it becomes clear to all the characters in the play that it is not this outward show, nor any temporary role that might have been adopted, that matters. As Petruchio says of Katherina:

Ha' done with words;
To me she's married, not unto my clothes.
(III.2.115-6)

It is the true and permanent character of the man that matters.

Just as the characters in the play are intended to learn as the play progresses so, by extension, are we, the audience. We are intended to realise that we must not trust to appearances alone, and there are many references throughout the play to the kind of illusions by which one may be deceived. Chief among these is the illusion of the play itself. As we have seen above, we are always aware that we are watching a play, and the actors not only play out other roles but also watch each other like an audience at a play:

LUCENTIO: But stay awhile, what company is this?
TRANIO: Master, some show to welcome us to town.
(I.1.46-7)

Petruchio brings together these two potential sources of illusion, clothing and plays, when he accuses the tailor of having made a theatrical costume for Katherina:

Thy gown? Why, ay. Come, tailor, let us see't.
O mercy, God! What masquing stuff is here?
(IV.3.86-7)

It is too easy to be deceived by appearances. Petruchio is not mad, nor is Katherina a witch; neither Lucentio nor Sly is in a dream, although each believes that he is. All of these characters are either acting out a part, pretending to be what they are not, or are deceived by the pretences of others. We know, as the lord knows, that none of these pretences can be acted out for ever and that reality must inevitably reassert itself. At the end of the play servants are back in control of their masters, Katherina has stated her obedience to Petruchio and, after the revelry and feasting, order is re-established and the accepted framework of society re-imposed.

It is not surprising that a play so much concerned with the education of its principal characters should include so many references to, and images from, education. Petruchio's 'taming-school' is shown to be more effective than the lessons given to Bianca by her tutors, and experience proves a better teacher than the academic study which Lucentio is intent on pursuing. Gremio comes from church 'As willingly as e'er I came from school' (II.2.149) and Lucentio persuades a Pedant to help him further his deceit. The whole play is full of allusions to education.

There are also a great many images of food. One of the ways in which Shakespeare establishes a festival atmosphere, at which strange events are likely, is to centre the play on a series of feasts, only one of which actually takes place. Sly is promised all sorts of delicacies in the Induction, but refuses them all in preference of a pot of small ale. Baptista arranges a wedding feast for Petruchio and Katherina, but his daughter is denied not only this feast, but any kind of food by her new husband. Baptista arranges another feast for the wedding of Tranio and Bianca and again his plans are frustrated. Finally all is resolved and the last feast, which all the lovers attend, is actually held.

There are a number of reasons for the prevalence of food images. In Act IV Scene 1, Petruchio explains his reasons for depriving both himself and Katherina of food:

I tell thee, Kate, 'twas burnt and dried away
And I expressly am forbid to touch it,
For it engenders choler, planteth anger;
And better 'twere that both of us did fast,
Since, of ourselves, ourselves are choleric,
Than feed it with such over-roasted flesh.
(IV.1.156–61)

Elizabethan medical theory believed that a good diet maintained the health of the body. Just as the sealing of the marriage between Katherina and Petruchio must be postponed until she has submitted to him, so the feasting must wait until Katherina is less proud, and this is best done by denying her food. Lucentio holds the feast in the last scene 'to close our stomachs up' and this adds another dimension to the imagery of feasting, for 'stomach' means pride as well as appetite and part of the function of this final feast is to demonstrate how well characters have overcome their pride. In her final speech Katherina warns the other wives:

I see our lances are but straws,
Our strength as weak, our weakness past compare,
That seeming to be most which we indeed least are,
Then vail your stomachs, for it is no boot. . . .
(V.2.172–5)

Since it is Petruchio's intention to change Katherina into a 'Kate' (a cake), it is appropriate that it should be at a feast that she demonstrates that her pride is conquered.

The play in performance

One indication of the success of *The Taming of the Shrew* lies in its popularity in the theatre and the number of adaptations which it has generated. *The Taming of a Shrew* was staged in 1594 and John Fletcher wrote a reply to Shakespeare's play called *The Woman's Prize, or The Tamer Tamed* some twenty-five years after Shakespeare's original. In 1667 an adaptation by John Lacy called *Sauny the Scot* which made Grumio the central character was seen and disliked by Samuel Pepys. The most celebrated re-working of the play was that by the actor David Garrick (1717–79) who pruned the text to produce a play called *Catherine and Petruchio* in 1754.

This adaptation formed the basis for Frederick Reynolds' opera in 1828, and a very different musical version of the play, Cole Porter's *Kiss Me Kate*, enjoyed considerable success when it was first produced in 1948. The most interesting of all adaptations is the recent work, *The Shrew*, by Charles Marowitz. This play uses selected scenes and speeches from *The Taming of the Shrew* (often in a different order from that of Shakespeare's play) interspersed with a modern love story. The effect of this adaptation is to illuminate some aspects of Petruchio's relationship with Katherina, and Marowitz's play is well worth reading.*

Shakespeare's own play has been performed very frequently in recent years, including notable productions for the Royal Shakespeare Company by John Barton in 1960 and by Michael Bogdanov in 1978.

---

*C. Marowitz, *The Shrew*, Calder and Boyar, London, 1975.

Part 4

Hints for study

Studying a play

In studying a dramatic text we need to use a different technique from that which we would employ in reading a novel or a poem. Almost all plays were written to be performed in front of an audience and to have an immediate effect on that audience. Therefore, even though our approach to the play as students of literature is to read the text very carefully indeed, we need also to be very aware of the way in which the dramatist communicates with his audience through other means than through his words alone.

For example, at the end of Act III Scene 2, Petruchio wishes to leave with his bride before the wedding feast. Katherina first entreats him to stay and then refuses to go with him. Petruchio seizes her and says:

> Nay, look not big, nor stamp, nor stare, nor fret,
> I will be master of what is mine own
> (III.2.227–8)

It is important to bear in mind that Petruchio is addressing these lines to Baptista and the others, pretending to believe that they are attacking Katherina and preventing her from leaving. In fact what is happening is that Katherina herself is fretting and stamping as she struggles by his side. A good deal of the humour of these lines comes from the contrast between the words and what is actually happening on the stage. We need to be aware of the actions and reactions of characters as well as of the words they speak.

Sometimes the mere presence of a particular character in a scene in which he may have very few lines can be of great significance. Thus, for example, in Act IV Scene 4 Baptista discusses the arrangements for Bianca's wedding with Tranio (whom he believes to be Lucentio) while the real Lucentio stands and listens to his every word. In this scene the presence of Lucentio in itself adds to the humour.

You should, therefore, bear in mind the following points as you read the text:

(1) Which characters are on stage in each scene?
(2) How might these characters be reacting to what is happening?
(3) Is the physical appearance or dress of the characters significant?

(4) How might the tone of voice of the actor affect the meaning of the lines?

For an illustration of these points, consider Act IV Scene 5 of the play. Petruchio, Katherina, Hortensio and an unspecified number of servants are on their way back to Padua from Petruchio's house. The clothes which Petruchio and Katherina wear are as significant in this scene as they are elsewhere in the play. Before their marriage they must both have been dressed in a manner typical of the ladies and gentlemen of the day. Petruchio, however, arrived fantastically dressed for the wedding and the visual contrast between his appearance and that of the other characters (especially his bride in all her finery) must have been very pronounced. At Petruchio's house Katherina has been very poorly dressed and, having been refused the dress which the tailor brought, she and Petruchio set off for Padua at the end of Act IV Scene 3 in their 'honest mean habiliments'.

Thus in Act IV Scene 5 Katherina and Petruchio are very poorly dressed and their strange appearance may well provoke a reaction from Vincentio when he encounters them. (You might like to consider how Katherina should be dressed in the final two scenes of the play and the kinds of reaction which this might provoke among the other characters in those scenes.)

The meeting with Vincentio allows great scope for the actress playing Katherina to indicate through her tone of voice whether or not she has been 'tamed' by Petruchio. Critics have disagreed widely about whether Katherina is submissive or not in this scene, and this degree of divergence is indicative of the scope which is given to the actress to interpret the part.*

In the first dozen lines of the scene Petruchio establishes the power he has over Katherina: if she refuses to agree with him (even when he is very obviously completely wrong) she will not go to her father's house. There is, however, a whole range of possibilities in the way in which Katherina reacts when she realises the extent of this power. Consider this speech:

> Forward, I pray, since we have come so far,
> And be it moon, or sun, or what you please.
> And if you please to call it a rush-candle,
> Henceforth I vow it shall be so for me.
> (IV.5.12–15)

What does this reveal of Katherina's attitude to Petruchio? Is she angry

*See, for example, Ralph Berry, *Shakespeare's Comedies*, Princeton University Press, Princeton, 1972; John Russell Brown, *Shakespeare and his Comedies*, Methuen, London, 1957; Hardin Craig, *An Interpretation of Shakespeare*, Citadel Press, New York, 1948; and P. Swinden, *An Introduction to Shakespeare's Comedies*, Macmillan, London, 1973.

and resentful? Is she prepared to do as he wishes for the time being? Is she now totally submissive and quite willing to do as Petruchio says? Is she so in love with Petruchio that she is happy to agree with him?

This speech could be made to convey any of these emotions: so much depends upon the way in which the particular actress delivers the lines.

The speech with which Katherina greets Vincentio later in this scene allows even further scope for the actress to make a choice in the true meaning of the lines. As well as the tone of her voice, her movements (whether or not, for example, she looks at Petruchio) may well be significant in delivering this speech:

> Young budding virgin, fair and fresh and sweet,
> Whither away, or where is thy abode?
> Happy the parents of so fair a child,
> Happier the man whom favourable stars
> Allots thee for his lovely bedfellow
>   (IV.5.36–41)

Think about the different ways in which this speech might be delivered.

Character and plot

Many of the essay questions set on dramatic texts are concerned with the way in which characters are portrayed or with the development of plot lines within the play.

In building up a character sketch of a particular individual in a play you need to bear in mind the following points:

(1) In what scenes does the character appear?
(2) What is said by the character?
(3) What is said to the character?
(4) What is said about the character?
(5) What is said about the character in those scenes in which the character does not appear?
(6) In what way might the character develop or change in the course of the play?

The last two points are very important and may require some further elaboration.

The audience or readers of a Shakespearean play are in the position of having more information than any of the characters in it. The entire action of the play takes place before the audience and therefore the audience knows much more about what is happening than any of the individual characters ever can. Thus, for example, the audience feels superior to poor Vincentio both in Act IV Scene 5 when he meets Katherina and in Act V Scene 1 when he is shut out of Lucentio's house.

We have seen the earlier scenes and are in possession of far more information than Vincentio and we can, therefore, make sense of actions which seem incomprehensible to him.

Bertrand Evans, in *Shakespeare's Comedies*, traces the ways in which Shakespeare uses this device of different levels of awareness on the part of audience and participant throughout his work.* One particular effect of this device is that the audience learn what opinions characters have of each other. We learn, for example, a great deal about Kate's reputation during Act I even though she herself is off-stage for most of this time. Very often, of course, reputations can be ill deserved, and you might consider how many characters have reputations which are proved to be unjustified.

Shakespeare's plays are generally concerned with education in that principal characters learn something of themselves in the course of the play which they had not realised before. It is for this reason that we should look for development and change in the characters in *The Taming of the Shrew*. There are many references to education and to change in the course of the play and you need to think about what the principal characters learn and how they change as the play goes on. You might divide up your notes as follows:

(1) What is the character like at the beginning of the play?
(2) What happens to change/educate the character?
(3) How does the character change? How is this change made clear to the audience?

A more detailed and extensive character study could consider, in addition to the points listed above, the kind of language used by the character. Very often in real life we are aware of the differences in the way in which people talk. We could probably recognise our friends with our eyes closed because we can identify their voices, particular phrases they are fond of, and their general manner of speech.

In a play characters are often more clearly identifiable by their speech than are people in real life. Petruchio, for example, speaks differently from Lucentio; Tranio speaks differently from Grumio. A detailed study would take these differences into account.

The play includes a number of characters who interact with each other and whose destinies are closely connected. The marriage of Bianca depends upon the marriage of her sister: their two futures are intertwined. A full study of any of the major characters, therefore, would include not only consideration of what happens to that character in the course of the play, but also some comparison with a similar character. Petruchio can be compared with Lucentio, for example; Lucentio

---

*B. Evans, *Shakespeare's Comedy*, Oxford University Press, London, 1960.

with his fellow 'tutor' Hortensio; Tranio with Grumio; Bianca with Katherina; and Baptista with Vincentio. Some of these possibilities are illustrated in the sample essay questions later in this section.

In examining the plot of the play it is useful to try to separate the two stories which combine to form the main action: the story of the courtship of Bianca and the story of the taming of Katherina. Make a list of the twelve scenes which form the main action of the play and note which of these are concerned exclusively with one of the two sisters and which with both plots. You might start like this:

BIANCA / KATHERINA

Act I Scene 1   concerned with *both* sisters. Baptista sets out the conditions of Bianca's marriage, stressing that Kate must marry first. All the suitors so far desire Bianca.

Notice also where the climaxes in the two plots occur. The marriage of Katherina is arranged in Act II and completed in Act III, yet there are issues in her relationship with Petruchio which still need to be resolved. The courtship of Bianca takes place more gradually and she is not married until Act V. Consider carefully the effect of having the two courtships taking place at different speeds. Notice also the contrast between adjacent scenes, or sometimes different parts of the same scene: for example, look at Act II Scene 1 where the courtship of Katherina is followed immediately by the bidding for Bianca. The effect here is to make Petruchio's strange wooing look less bizarre by following it with an equally comic auction. Notice carefully the order of the scenes and think about the way in which our view of any particular scene is affected by the scene immediately before it. A diagram like this might be helpful:

Act I Scene 1	Master and servant	Kate's extreme behaviour	Lucentio in love
Act I Scene 2	Master and servant	Petruchio's extreme behaviour	Petruchio in love

Sample essay questions

(1) In what ways do the Christopher Sly scenes introduce the main action of the play?

(2) Compare and contrast the relationships which Grumio and Tranio have with their masters.

(3) How are the characters of Lucentio and Petruchio introduced and contrasted in Act I of the play?

(4) Compare and contrast the changes in the characters of Katherina and Bianca during the course of the play.

(5) On the evidence presented in the play does Katherina appear to be a suitable wife for Petruchio?

(6) Illustrate some of the ways in which Shakespeare reminds us that we are spectators watching a play.

(7) Compare and contrast the characters of Baptista and Gremio.

(8) Illustrate the ability which Petruchio has to vary his language according to the needs of the situation.

(9) To what extent are the major images of the play connected with its theme?

(10) Why is Act IV Scene 5 a crucial scene in the play?

(11) Illustrate the different kinds of humour employed in Act IV Scene 1 and Act IV Scene 3 of *The Taming of the Shrew*.

Answering an essay question

Students answering essay questions frequently make the mistake of failing to read the question sufficiently carefully. They may see a question about *The Taming of the Shrew* and proceed to write all they can remember about the play. This is a very poor technique and you will lose marks for writing down irrelevant material. Read the question carefully and work out what particular aspect of the play is being identified as the focus of the question. Although in other essays you may have been advised to write an introduction and a conclusion you will not always have the time available to do this in answering an examination essay. Thus, in answering question (3) given above, for example, it might be best to go straight into the answer, like this: 'We first meet Lucentio in conversation with his servant Tranio . . ..'

In the main body of your answer you should aim to show your knowledge of the text and your understanding of what it means. Therefore you should not only cite quotations from the play but also explain what the quotation is being used to illustrate, in this way:

In his soliloquy at the end of Act IV Scene 1, Petruchio reveals to the audience his plan to tame Kate. He refers to her as a hawk, 'My falcon is now sharp and passing empty', showing that he intends to master her by treating her as one would a wild creature in order to subdue her.

Sample answer

(1) *In what ways do the Christopher Sly scenes introduce the main action of the play?*

One function of the Sly Induction scenes is to frame the main action of the play. Sly and his 'lady' are established as spectators of the comedy which unfolds in Padua and, thus, the story of Petruchio, Lucentio, Katherina and Bianca becomes a play-within-a-play acted to Sly, who is himself an actor watched by the real audience in the theatre. Within the main plot, characters are frequently seen to act as spectators to the actions of others: for example, in Act I Scene 1 Tranio and Lucentio stand and watch as Baptista explains to Gremio and the others the conditions governing the marriage of his daughters. Later, in Act V Scene 1, Petruchio and Katherina become the audience as they 'stand aside and see the end of this controversy', that is, the confusion over the identity of Vincentio. Since the main plot so often relies on characters acting as spectators it is appropriate that it should open with an actor-spectator, Sly.

Sly is shown in the first lines of the play to be concerned about his social standing. Although he later admits to being no more than a wandering tinker, he professes to having noble ancestors who 'came in with Richard Conqueror'. A number of characters in the main plot are concerned not to have their social status undervalued: Bianca in Act II Scene 1 is afraid of being made a 'slave', and one of the reasons Hortensio abandons his courtship of Bianca is that he thinks she has no sense of social status, and prefers a servant to a gentleman: 'such a one as leaves a gentleman/And makes a god of such a cullion' (IV.2).

The lord who finds Sly asleep 'practises' on Sly, playing a trick on him to make him forget who he really is. This introduces the very prevalent use of disguises and tricks in the main body of the play. For example, Tranio tricks the pedant into thinking that his life is in danger and disguises him as Vincentio. Furthermore, Sly is given a very great social elevation for a brief, finite spell of time and is able to command someone (the lord) who is, in fact, superior to him. In the main plot Tranio finds himself in a similar situation, changing places with Lucentio for a brief period, able to give orders (a fact which Biondello finds very amusing in Act IV Scene 4). He knows that this situation will not last long, that he is being used by his master 'like a greyhound/Which runs himself, and catches for his master' (V.2). We do not see Sly coming to the same realisation but it is implied that he will eventually find himself changed back into Sly again and put back into the cold: his temporary elevation is for the amusement of the lord.

While Sly is in the lord's house he is provided with a 'wife', the disguised page Bartholomew. There are to be three marriages in the main plot of the play and Sly's 'wedding' forms an ironic preface. His wife appears to be an ideal wife of the type for whom Petruchio, Lucentio and Hortensio are searching: 'My husband and my lord, my lord and husband,/I am your wife in all obedience' (Induction 2).

It appears that 'she' is submissive and accepts the superiority of her 'husband'. In fact, of course, the speaker is a false wife and not at all what she seems to be. The play as a whole is to demonstrate how deceptive appearances can be, that those dressed as tutors may, in fact, be gentlemen, and that the apparently submissive Bianca may turn into the 'veriest shrew' herself.

Most of the changes in character and in outward appearance in the main part of the play are brought about by love and we are introduced to the power of love to effect change in the Induction, through the pictures which adorn the walls of the lord's house. Their subjects are taken from the works of Ovid and are all concerned with the metamorphoses brought about through love. The biggest 'change' brought about in the main plot of the play is the apparent transformation of Katherina, such that her father exclaims at the end of the play: 'she is changed, as she had never been' (V.2).

There are some incidental similarities between the Induction and the main plot, for example, the references to the gentlemanly pastimes of hawking and hunting in both, but perhaps more striking is the fact that the consummation of Sly's marriage has to be postponed until the play is ended, just as the kiss which seals Petruchio's marriage to Katherina is delayed until her ritual 'taming'. The last time we hear from Sly he is falling asleep and this may well remind us that, before the end of the play, Katherina is to be deprived of sleep as part of her 'taming'.

One final irony links together the main plot and the Induction. The players are themselves deluded by the lord, who tells them, 'There is a lord will hear you play tonight' (Induction 1), carefully failing to reveal Sly's true social position. Thus the whole of the main plot is acted under false pretences and becomes the largest instance of trickery in a play which abounds in minor deceits and lies.

This answer was written by following a simple essay plan, prepared in advance in note form. The plan looked like this:

(a) Sly's concern for status
(b) greyhounds
(c) trick on Sly—disguised as lord for brief time
(d) Sly taken from cold to warmth
(e) Sly's obedient 'wife'
(f) description of lord's house

(g) exchange of master and servant
(h) pictures of Metamorphosis
(k) postponement of 'wedding'
(l) Sly as audience
(m) lord's lies to the players
(n) Sly falls asleep
(o) Sly's language

This is a list of features in the Induction which can be linked with corresponding features in the main action of the play. The order of the list is roughly that in which the features occur in the Induction. In developing this plan into an essay it is necessary to observe the following:

(1) Not all the points in the list are of equal significance. The fact that there are references to greyhounds both in the Induction and in the main play probably does not matter so much as, say, the kind of wife which Sly is given.

(2) Decide which are your major points and devote the bulk of your essay to these. Indicate to your reader that you are aware that some of your observations are merely of secondary interest by grouping them together and dealing with them briefly.

(3) Do not dwell too long or too elaborately on any single point because this will reduce the time you have for the rest of the essay. For example, it would have been possible to cite laboriously all the instances of disguise in the play in dealing with point (c) in the essay plan, but it is preferable to select a single clear example and move on to the next point.

(4) There may be points listed in the essay plan which cannot be used at all because of the pressures of time and space. For example, in this essay a comparison might have been made between the description of the lord's house in the Induction and Gremio's house in Act II Scene 1. Furthermore, it would have been possible to refer to the mixture of different kinds of language in the Induction and demonstrate a similar variety within the main action of the play. Both of these features would have been relevant to the essay, but neither was included because there were other more significant points to be made. Often it is impossible to use some ideas which would be relevant because of the pressures of time.

Part 5

Suggestions for further reading

The text

HARRISON, G. B. (ED.): *The Taming of the Shrew*, Penguin Books, Harmondsworth, 1951. This includes a useful summary of the play.

HEILMAN, R. B. (ED.): *The Taming of the Shrew*, (The Signet Classic Shakespeare) New American Library, London, 1966. This includes extracts from selected criticisms.

HIBBARD, G. R. (ED.): *The Taming of the Shrew*, (The New Penguin Shakespeare) Penguin Books, Harmondsworth, 1968. This is the text used in these Notes.

THOMPSON, ANN (ED.): *The Taming of the Shrew*, (The New Cambridge Shakespeare) Cambridge University Press, Cambridge, 1984.

Other works by Shakespeare

ALEXANDER, P. (ED.): *The Complete Works*, Collins, London and Glasgow, 1951; paperback edition, HarperCollins, Glasgow, 1994. There are countless editions of Shakespeare's collected works. This is a convenient single-volume edition with a reliable text and a brief but informative introduction.

The plays most relevant to *The Taming of the Shrew* are probably *The Comedy of Errors* (for the reasons outlined above in Part 3), *All's Well That Ends Well* (for a woman's role in marriage), and *Much Ado About Nothing* (for reluctant lovers who eventually marry).

General works on Shakespeare

There are many general works on Shakespeare, of which the following are useful and, at present, up to date:

BAYLEY, PETER: *An A·B·C of Shakespeare*, (Longman York Handbooks) Longman, Harlow, 1985. New edition, 1993. A general reference book, alphabetically arranged.

CAMPBELL, O. J. and QUINN, E. G. (EDS): *A Shakespeare Encyclopaedia*, Methuen, London, 1966. This is also arranged alphabetically and deals with Shakespeare's life, works and times.

HALLIDAY, F. E.: *A Shakespeare Companion 1564–1964*, Penguin Books, Harmondsworth, 1964.

JARDINE, L.: *Still Harping on Daughters*, Harvester Press, Brighton, 1981, reprinted 1983. Places Shakespeare's treatment of women in the context of contemporary drama and criticism.

LLOYD EVANS, G. and B.: *Everyman's Companion to Shakespeare*, Dent, London, 1978. This includes a useful glossary, a list of all the characters in Shakespeare's plays and a good section on Elizabethan theatre. It attempts to sort out some of the facts of Shakespeare's life and separate them from the myths and legends that have grown up.

MUIR, K. and SCHOENBAUM, S. (EDS): *A New Companion to Shakespeare Studies*, Cambridge University Press, London, 1971. This contains eighteen articles, those on the Elizabethan stage and Shakespeare's reading being the most relevant to *The Taming of the Shrew*.

Dictionaries

The standard reference work on the meaning of English words in the past is the *Oxford English Dictionary*. However, for students the glossary in *Everyman's Companion to Shakespeare* may suffice. In addition, the following is a convenient source of information:

ONIONS, C. T.: *A Shakespeare Glossary*, Oxford University Press, London, 1911, revised by Robert D. Eagleson, 1986.

Criticism

There are a great many books on Shakespearean comedy, all of which have something to say on *The Taming of the Shrew*. The following is a selection which you may find particularly useful:

BERRY, R.: *Shakespeare's Comedies*, Princeton University Press, Princeton, 1972. This sees Bianca as becoming increasingly shrewish as the play goes on.

BROWN, JOHN RUSSELL: *Shakespeare and his Comedies*, Methuen, London, 1957. This deals very fully with the financial aspects of marriage in the play.

CHAMPION, L. S.: *The Evaluation of Shakespeare's Comedy*, Harvard University Press, Cambridge, Mass., 1970. This sees Kate as unreformed at the end, merely re-directing her venom at the widow.

CHARLTON, H. B.: *Shakespearean Comedy*, Methuen, London, 1938. Generally concerned with the development from Latin to Italian to Elizabethan comedy, Charlton concentrates on the Bianca plot which he claims is not romantic.

DUSINBERE, J.: *Shakespeare and the Nature of Women*, Macmillan, London, 1975. A good introduction to feminist readings of the plays.

EDENS, W. (ED.): *Teaching Shakespeare*, Princeton University Press, Princeton, 1977. This includes two relevant chapters: D. M. Bergeron, 'Plays within Plays in Shakespeare's Early Comedies' and W. Schleiner, 'De-romanticizing the Shrew'.

EVANS, B.: *Shakespeare's Comedy*, Oxford University Press, London, 1960. The general aim of this book is to examine the way in which the audience generally has more knowledge than the participants. In *The Taming of the Shrew*, Evans suggests, this device is not as fully exploited as it might be.

HILLMAN, R.: *Shakespearean Subversions: The Trickster and the Play-Text*, Routledge, London, 1992. Includes a chapter on *The Taming of the Shrew*.

LEGGATT, A.: *Shakespeare's Comedy of Love*, Methuen, London, 1974. The contrast between the taming-school and the tuition of Bianca is emphasised.

SALINGAR, L.: *Shakespeare and the Traditions of Comedy*, Cambridge University Press, Cambridge, 1974. A very full account of the development of comedy from its origin up to Shakespeare. It illustrates the way in which Shakespeare improved upon *Supposes*.

SWINDEN, P.: *An Introduction to Shakespeare's Comedies*, Macmillan, London, 1973. Swinden points out that courtship is hardly mentioned in *The Comedy of Errors* but becomes much more significant in *The Taming of the Shrew*.

TILLYARD, E. M. W.: *Shakespeare's Early Comedies*, Chatto and Windus, London, 1965. This has a very good introductory chapter on comedy in general and a sensible account of *The Taming of the Shrew*.

TRAVERSI, D.: *Shakespeare: The Early Comedies*, Writers and Their Work 129, Longman, London, revised edition 1964. This suggests that Katherina might have good reason for being shrewish.

WALLER, G. (ED.): *Shakespeare's Comedies*, (Longman Critical Readers) Longman, 1991. Although quite sophisticated in its approach, this is a good survey of critical perspectives on Shakespearean comedy, and includes a chapter specifically on *The Taming of the Shrew*.

WELD, J.: *Meaning and Comedy*, State University of New York Press, Albany, 1975. This work deals fully with the metaphors of dreaming and acting within *The Taming of the Shrew*.

WELLS, S. (ED.): *Shakespeare Survey*, 37, Cambridge University Press, Cambridge, 1984. A volume dedicated to discussion of the early comedies.

Sources of the play

BULLOUGH, G. (ED.): *Narrative and Dramatic Sources of Shakespeare*, *I*, Routledge and Kegan Paul, London, 1961.

MUIR, K.: *The Sources of Shakespeare's Plays*, Methuen, London, 1977.

Background reading

BARROLL, J. L. (ED.): *The Revels History of Drama in English*, Vol III, 1576–1613, Methuen, London, 1975. A useful account of the theatrical history of the period.

CRAIG, HARDIN: *The Enchanted Glass: Elizabethan Mind in Literature*, Oxford University Press, New York, 1936; reissued by Blackwell, Oxford, 1950.

GURR, A.: *The Shakespearean Stage 1574–1642*, Cambridge University Press, Cambridge, 1970. A detailed and comprehensive account of the theatre in Shakespeare's time.

THOMPSON, P.: *Sir Thomas Wyatt and his Background*, Stanford University Press, Stanford, 1964. This includes a useful chapter on courtly love as a literary tradition and as practised in reality.

TILLYARD, E. M. W.: *The Elizabethan World Picture*, Chatto, London, 1943; reissued by Penguin, Harmondsworth, 1963.